# Farewell, My Colony

For 16 years Todd Crowell lived and worked in Hong Kong as a senior writer for *Asiaweek*, the leading English-language news magazine in Asia, owned by Time Inc. He covered the handover for *Asiaweek* and for the *Christian Science Monitor* newspaper. He currently lives in Japan.

# Farewell, My Colony

*Last Days in the Life of British Hong Kong*

Todd Crowell

**BLACKSMITH BOOKS**

ISBN 978-988-77928-0-2
Published by Blacksmith Books
Unit 26, 19/F, Block B, Wah Lok Industrial Centre,
31–35 Shan Mei St, Fo Tan, Hong Kong
*www.blacksmithbooks.com*

Typeset in Adobe Garamond by Alan Sargent
Printed in Hong Kong

First printing 2017
Portions of this book first appeared in *Asiaweek*
and the *Christian Science Monitor*

*For my wife, Setsuko, and for my colleagues at* Asiaweek, *whose minds I picked even when they didn't know they were being picked.*

# Contents

# Preface to the 2017 edition

As THE SWINGING seventies gave way to the more anxious 1980s, people in Hong Kong became increasingly apprehensive about the once comfortably distant date—July 1st 1997—when the 99-year lease on Hong Kong's hinterland, the "New" Territories, acquired in 1898, would expire.

Many businessmen were growing anxious about the impact this impending change would have on business basics: could their own land leases be extended beyond that date (virtually all land in Hong Kong then, as now, is "crown" land and leased, not sold, by the government)? Would other contracts be honored? More to the point: What did China intend to do with Hong Kong?

It was against this background that British Prime Minister Margaret Thatcher made her famous first visit to Beijing in September, 1982, to begin negotiating the future of the British colony.

Thatcher hoped to persuade China's leaders that continuing British administration of the territory was necessary for the stability and prosperity of Hong Kong. The chaos of the Cultural Revolution, which essentially ended only with Mao Zedong's death in 1976, was still a vivid memory; China's opening and "paramount leader" Deng Xiaoping's economic reforms were only just beginning.

She knew relatively little about China or Hong Kong, although she was undoubtedly briefed that China did not recognize as valid the 19th-century treaties that had ceded Hong Kong Island and the tip of Kowloon peninsula to Britain "in perpetuity" after the Opium Wars. She must also have known that Hong Kong could not continue as a viable entity without the New Territories.

The prime minister, however, seemed to think she had a duty to at least try to uphold the treaties that she claimed were still valid under international law.

For his part, Deng was unmovable on the notion that China would assume full sovereignty of the entire territory. Anything less would make him complicit in the treasonous territorial giveaways of the late Qing dynasty. Otherwise, he was willing to grant generous concessions guaranteeing Hong Kong's way of life and liberties post-1997 under his now famous but then novel "one country, two systems" formula, that was calculated to demonstrate to Taiwan that it could also safely reunify with the motherland.

Much was made following Mrs. Thatcher's death of how the "Iron Lady" had met her match in Deng. This is unfortunate. To be sure Deng, a former revolutionary war commander, was a tough hombre. But in truth Thatcher had a weak hand, which she was smart enough to understand. As the British would say, continued colonial administration of Hong Kong was just not on.

It took two more years of difficult negotiations for the British to finally come around to this position. They were trying times. In October, 1983, when it appeared that negotiations might collapse, the Hong Kong dollar began to plunge in value. That led to the pegging of the currency at 7.8 to the US dollar, a peg that continues to this day.

In 1984 London formally agreed it would surrender sovereignty over the entire territory, and in December, 1984 Thatcher made her second trip to Beijing to formally sign the Joint Declaration with Premier Zhao Ziyang at a ceremony in the Great Hall of the People.

Thatcher had been out of office for seven years when the actual transition ceremony took place at midnight June 30, 1997, so she didn't have to sit on the dais and watch the Union flag lowered for the last time. That role fell to newly minted Prime Minister Tony Blair. She was probably happy to be out of it.

In 2007 Thatcher gave an interview that expressed "regret" that she could not have persuaded China to accept continued British rule. But there is no shame in playing a leading part in what was one of the most enlightened yet practical acts of diplomacy in modern times. It gave Hong Kong people far more autonomy over their affairs than any of the so-called "autonomous regions" in China proper.

Those heady days leading up to the moment when the British Union flag was lowered for the last time, replaced by the red banner of China are etched on the memory of all Hongkongers who lived though it with varying degrees of trepidation and even eager anticipation. I recorded it as it happened for the first edition of this book in 1998. This new edition supplements the story with an afterword from the perspective of 20 years later.

# Introduction

IN LATE 1994 THE CHINESE GOVERNMENT erected a large digital clock in Tiananmen Square in the heart of Beijing. It started marking off the days—indeed, the seconds—until the moment when the British Union flag would be hauled down forever and the red, five-star flag of China hoisted over Hong Kong ending more than a century-and-a-half of British colonial rule. By my count there are three similar clocks: in the Great Hall of the People, at the Hong Kong border crossing at Lo Wu, and in the headquarters of the future Hong Kong garrison of the People's Liberation Army in the border city of Shenzhen, attesting to the importance the Chinese place on this event. Significantly, none could be found in Hong Kong, even though every one of the colony's more than six million people counted off the days with varying degrees of trepidation or in some cases, eager anticipation.

I arrived in Hong Kong in June 1987, exactly ten years before the handover and only three years after the British and Chinese governments had signed the Joint Declaration of 1984, agreeing to return the colony to China on July 1, 1997, the expiry date of its 99-year lease to the vast (by Hong Kong proportions) hinterland still known as the "New" Territories. In that agreement several promises were made that were to be repeated many times in the ensuing years. One was that Hong Kong would preserve its capitalist system for the next 50 years. Another was that Hong Kong people would enjoy an unprecedented autonomy over their own affairs, even after the territory returned to Chinese sovereignty. It was summed up under the late Chinese leader Deng Xiaoping's famous formula: "one country, two systems".

At the time, the handover seemed comfortably distant. Whether these promises would be kept, indeed whether they could be kept, was mostly theoretical. Even then, of course, anxieties and doubts circulated. Soon after I arrived, *Asiaweek*'s literary editor resigned and moved to Toronto. Over the years a constant stream of people have left for Australia, Canada and America. Often this involved long family separations while the breadwinner stayed behind to earn money and the rest of the family established a beachhead in North America or some other place of potential refuge. Many of them eventually returned to the colony having obtained their "travel insurance" should things go wrong.

The anxiety level increased exponentially when on June 4, 1989, Deng sent troops into Beijing to recapture Tiananmen Square from student demonstrators, killing hundreds, perhaps thousands. On that date I stood on an overpass in Causeway Bay and watched as tens of thousands of Hong Kong people, wearing white clothes of mourning or carrying black flags, marched silently through the streets past the New China News Agency, China's unofficial embassy, known in Chinese as Xinhua. The long-term effect of Tiananmen was not just to raise fears among Hongkongers that the tanks might one day rumble down Queen's Road—although there is an element of that, of course. It was more a shift in attitude in China toward Hong Kong. Suddenly, the territory no longer looked like a fat, complacent goose, content to sit quietly and lay golden eggs. This goose had a brain and feelings and the determination to stand up to the Chinese authorities. The next big shake-up came with the arrival in July 1992 of a new British governor, Christopher Patten. In October of that year he unveiled a plan to expand the number of democratically elected seats in the territory's legislature. Two years followed of acrimonious and ultimately fruitless negotiations with the Chinese before Patten went ahead with his plans and established a new electoral system.

Not everything happening, however, was high political drama. During those ten years it seemed that the British slowly, almost imperceptibly, began to fade away. The queen's profile disappeared from the face of the coins, replaced by the picture of the official flower. The last regular British Army battalion left Stanley Fort and flew back home. When I arrived, such senior posts of chief secretary, chief justice of the supreme court, financial secretary, were all held by Britons. As the countdown clock started ticking, these posts were all filled by ethnic Chinese, though often very British in their own ways. Even the chief steward of the Royal Hong Kong Jockey Club was Chinese. Slowly this most Chinese of colonies was becoming "sinofied" in every way.

This book is an attempt to tell, and, in some way, to interpret Hong Kong's last two years under British rule. It was the critical time when the institutions to implement the "one country, two systems" concept were put in place. It is not meant to be an insider's account; I had no special access. I am not in a position to write authoritatively on the history of the negotiations leading up to the Joint Declaration or to comment on whether the British could have obtained better terms. My feeling is that they got the best deal they could. I am more interested in looking forward and speculating on the shape of Hong Kong to come based on my own close observation of the events preceding the change of sovereignty. I will do so as the book progresses. And being American, neither Chinese nor British, I can look on the unfolding events with some dispassion. I turned this manuscript in to my publisher in late July 1997, and since then I have made no changes or additions other than to correct minor inaccuracies such as the spelling of names. I've made no attempt to rewrite history in the light of later events. If some of my predictions were wrong, they none the less represent the spirit, hopes and anxieties of the moment.

Like many people who live here, I am often asked what will happen to Hong Kong after 1997. Am I an optimist or a pessimist? Surely, as this narrative intends to show, the notion of one country two systems, attractive as it sounds in concept, is difficult to put into practice. Yet some things can be said with confidence about life and Hong Kong's future after 1997. First, Beijing sincerely wants Hong Kong to succeed, mainly on the terms in which it has always succeeded, as an entrepôt and prosperous and vital window to the outside world. China's leaders cannot let it be said that the place went to pot soon after the British left. That would be a blow too terrible to contemplate.

I also think that Beijing honestly wants to implement its promise to let Hong Kong people run their own affairs with considerable leeway, but they worry that Hong Kong may meddle in and destabilize China. That may seem far-fetched. Hong Kong represents only 0.5 percent of China's 1.2 billion people. But they are comparatively wealthy, have traveled widely, are broadly educated, have imbibed many Western, liberal and democratic values. Many of them hold foreign citizenship and thus the added assurance that they can leave if the heat gets too great. Beijing worries that they will spread these values beyond their own borders to undermine their regime or at the least embarrass them internationally. Thus China will be under constant temptation to clamp down. It will take considerable restraint and wisdom to resist this impulse.

China's leaders would have liked to turn the clock back to 1984, the year the Joint Declaration was signed. Beijing liked Hong Kong as it was then—the Hong Kong it *thought* it was getting in 1997. This was the Hong Kong with a strong executive government, an appointed and compliant legislature, a generally passive population. Strong laws existed to control social unrest, and if they were lightly applied, they were still on the books. Through its appointed, temporary legislature, Beijing will do what it can to roll back some, but not all, of the democratic reforms. It will also strengthen some of the police laws that were relaxed after Tiananmen. But it is too late to turn the clock back totally—Hong Kong's political sophistication and awareness has been awakened beyond the recognition of anyone who lived here even ten years ago.

# September 1995      -652 DAYS

*"Hello, I'm Yeung Sum, your legislative councillor."*

HONG KONG IS IN THE GRIP OF AN ELECTION. Political posters cover the landscape. People thrust flyers in my hands as I board my morning bus. Candidates receive lengthy stories and profiles in the newspapers. For the first time, every one of the 60 seats in the colonial legislature (known here as the Legislative Council, or "Legco") is to be elected, albeit in some cases from very small electorates of a few hundred or even a few dozen voters. From my bus window I spot the poster promoting one Samuel Wong with the inspiring slogan, ENGINEERING A BETTER HONG KONG. Where else but in Hong Kong would somebody use such a clunker of a slogan? But where else but Hong Kong could one find an electoral district made up entirely of civil engineers?

Two weeks before the polling I followed my Legco member as he trotted down the dank concrete corridor of a public housing estate in Aberdeen canvassing for votes. To cover the sixteen floors in this public housing estate, he had to move quickly. Every few yards he paused to shake hands through the metal gratings that guard each door. "Hello, I'm Yeung Sum, your legislative councillor. I helped to stop the labor importation scheme," he repeated at every door. Meanwhile, his young aides, wearing vests with the green colors of the Democratic Party, handed out leaflets and took down telephone numbers of potential supporters.

Yeung Sum represents the south side of Hong Kong Island, the territory's "Riviera", where apartments in Repulse Bay, popular with American expatriates, rent for more than US$10,000 a month. But he has lower-income constituents, too. They are worried about the government's proposal to allow more foreign construction workers into the territory. Many of the residents of this public housing estate, home to fishermen operating from nearby Aberdeen Harbour, belong to guilds supported by the Chinese government. Many probably back Yeung's opponent, Cheng Kai-nam, of the Democratic Alliance for the Betterment of Hong Kong. Yeung Sum is vice chairman of the Democratic Party led by the legendary pro-democracy leader Martin Lee. His opponent in this race holds exactly the same position in the main pro-Beijing party. Polls have indicated that the race is close; Yeung has to hustle.

I asked about the issues in this campaign. Yeung says that people in his district are concerned about rising unemployment, maintenance of the public housing estates and that Hong Kong perennial, rising bus fares. But the great political divide is really between those usually labeled "pro-democracy", and those lumped in the "pro-Beijing" camp. Broadly speaking, the pro-democracy advocates seek the widest representation in an independent legislature as the best way of preserving Hong Kong's promised autonomy and freedoms after the change of sovereignty. The pro-Beijing camp argues that the territory's best interests are served by accommodating, not confronting, China.

After following this parade for several floors, I decided I had learned enough about campaigning Hong Kong-style. Before I left, I took the candidate aside and asked him, "given that China strongly dislikes your politics, do you expect to be able to run again after 1997?"

"It depends," he replied soberly. "I don't see any reason why not unless I'm barred for being 'unpatriotic'." An official of the Hong Kong and Macau Affairs Office had recently stated that future candidates must be "patriotic" and "loyal".

"It would be difficult for China to bar popular politicians from running again because it would be a shock to the community. But I'm confident I'll be elected again," and he turned and trotted down the corridor to shake some more hands.

On election day, September 18, 1995, I voted too, even though I am an American. I hadn't planned to vote—somehow it didn't seem right to interfere in another country's politics. But some people from the government came to my apartment to ask me to register; it seemed impolite to say no. And, in the end, it proved irresistible. This was, after all, an historic election, and after eight years' residence in Hong Kong, I qualified as an elector. But then nationality never counted for much in this place. In one of the constituencies on Hong Kong Island, the three candidates were British, Canadian and Australian—all ethnic Chinese, of course. I know this because the newspapers print each candidate's passport along with other useful background information such as age, profession and political affiliation—as in "Anthony Wong, 35, Attorney, British Dependent Territories Passport with Australian residency".

I could have voted twice, but I never figured out which functional constituency I belonged in. As a writer, I should have also asked for an extra ballot in something called the "Community, Social and Personal Services" constituency along with the race horse jockeys, bar hostesses and other pillars of the community. Or, perhaps it was the Transportation and Communications Constituency along with the taxi drivers. Every working person in Hong Kong, which means just about everybody, gets to choose two legislators, one from a geographical district, just like the state legislature or British parliament, and another from a bewildering list of constituencies grouped around occupations: garment and textile workers, assembly line workers, and so on. Adding to the confusion are the older electoral districts built around professions, which means that some people have three votes. Say you are an accountant. First you vote for your local member, then for the candidate of the "Financial, Insurance, Real Estate and Business Services" functional constituency. Then there is one just for accountants.

When the Joint Declaration returning Hong Kong to China was signed in 1984, not one Legco member was elected by anyone. Part of the body was made up of "officials", that is, civil servants, with the rest appointed by the governor. That situation had prevailed for most of the colony's 154-year history. When I arrived in 1987, a small measure of democracy had been introduced. Some members were chosen by the partly elected district and urban councils (small local governing boards). Others were returned through a system of so-called functional constituencies. There was one for lawyers (held by Democratic Party leader Martin Lee for a long time), doctors, accountants, teachers and so on. At most, about 25,000 people held the franchise out of a total of more than five million.

Even then a debate was raging over how much democracy to allow. It was a question for the committee drafting Hong Kong's post-1997 constitution, called the Basic Law. It was also a matter of negotiation between China and Britain. The government went through an elaborate, and some felt disingenuous, exercise in canvassing public opinion. About that time China's then Foreign Minister Wu Xueqian flew into the territory for consultations. One of my earliest impressions is the picture of a grim-faced Governor Sir David Wilson, greeting the foreign minister at his country estate at Fanling. Soon thereafter, the authorities suddenly concluded that Hong Kong's people were not ready for more democracy, discounting thousands of petitions to the contrary. Direct elections originally scheduled for 1988 were canceled and protesters scolded for rocking the boat. The first real direct elections were not held until 1991.

That was the year that Yeung Sum won his seat in a landslide vote for what were then known as the United Democrats. They and their liberal allies carried thirteen out of the eighteen seats contested openly. But the legislature still had an overwhelming contingent of members holding their seats by virtue of the office they held or by appointment from the governor. These were slated to disappear in 1995, when the number of direct seats would increase marginally to 20 with the remainder indirectly elected or chosen by restricted franchises. These legislators would, as the local parlance had it, ride the "through train" past 1997 until the first elections under Chinese rule in 1999. This was a comforting metaphor for the continuity of institutions from one era to another. The fateful year 1997 is the station where no one wants to stop. On board the passengers would nap, read or play mahjong, as "1997" passes by barely noticed. This was supposed to reinforce that nebulous but eminently desirable thing called "confidence".

That was the situation when Christopher Patten arrived in 1992. Hong Kong had never seen anything like him. Soon he was canvassing the public housing estates like he was looking for votes in his old parliamentary constituency in Bath. His defeat by a Liberal Democrat in the 1992 British general election had steered him Hong Kong's way instead of into Prime Minister John Major's cabinet (for which he might be grateful—the governor's pay is better, and it is tax free). Then in his first major speech in October, he outlined an ambitious plan for expanding democratic representation.

It is widely but incorrectly believed that Patten introduced democracy into Hong Kong. As we have seen, universal suffrage was in place during the 1991 election. All Patten did to expand the voting rolls was to lower the voting age from 21 to 18. The problem was that all of those votes were channeled into a small number of seats in the total body. What Patten did was to take the employment rolls, divide them by nine and call them "functional constituencies". In doing so, he effectively gave everyone two votes and expanded the number of seats in the legislature chosen from a mass franchise to half of the body.

He presented these as "proposals", but the Chinese side never accepted them. Two years of negotiations proved fruitless. Beijing refused to budge from its position that Britain had shown bad faith in introducing and later pushing through the legislature a new electoral system without its prior consultation or approval. To listen to Beijing, it was the worst example of British perfidy since the Opium Wars. It opened a fissure between the last governor and China that was never bridged. Though Patten visited Beijing once, he never met with its top leaders, never heard a good word in the Chinese press, which piled on the verbal abuse calling him everything from a "whore" or a "sinner of a thousand iniquities" or other choice epithets. The governor usually gave as good as he got, treating Chinese critics as if they were junior shadow ministers on the opposition benches of the House of Commons. In his last year in office, as it became clear the Chinese would dismantle his political reforms, he seemed to become more and more sarcastic.

Beijing announced it would simply disband Patten's legislature on July 1 and replace it with a temporary body that came to be called the "provisional legislature". Early on the morning of the election, Beijing issued a stern reminder that it would undo the work of the voters, a major public relations blunder that probably cost sympathetic candidates dearly. The through train had run off the rails. Instead of cruising past the 1997 station, it would come to a screeching halt. The conductor would arouse everyone from their slumbers and make them get out of the train and stand on the platform while a new group of passengers clambered on board.

A few weeks after the election, Hong Kong's "incredible shrinking governor", Chris Patten, stood tall for a few hours as he delivered his next-to-last policy address to the new Legislative Council. That cutting sobriquet had been pinned on him by Sir Percy Cradock in a radio interview from London the day before. Patten, he said, was "rapidly being marginalized as the Chinese and British governments work together to reduce the damage that his reforms have done." Sir Percy, of course, is the foreign-office diplomat and former ambassador to Beijing who helped negotiate the Joint Declaration of 1984, which returns Hong Kong—all of it, not just the leased New Territories—to China in 1997. Thus he is, depending on your point of view: (1) the architect of one of the best recent examples of pragmatic modern diplomacy, or, (2) the man who sold Hong Kong down the river.

Bad blood has flowed between the two ever since Patten first unveiled his plan to expand democracy in the territory. Cradock comes from the old school of China specialists, invariably labeled "mandarins", who have provided most of the colony's recent governors. Patten's predecessor was of the type. Sir David (now

Lord) Wilson was a China specialist, Mandarin language speaker and scholar who had served with the British mission during the Cultural Revolution, whereas Patten is a former Conservative party politician who cheerfully admits he didn't know chop sticks from chop suey when he took office. But Britain's Prime Minister John Major had grown wary of the mandarins, whom he thought were too deferential to Beijing. So when Patten, as Conservative Party chairman, engineered Major's re-election in 1992 but lost his own seat in parliament, he obviously was due a plum reward. Would it be a safe seat and cabinet post, elevation to the House of Lords or possibly governorship of faraway Hong Kong?

Just before the governor's speech I slipped into the public gallery to watch the new legislators take their oaths of office. Nobody bothered to check my bag, and no metal detectors barred my passage—such is the innocence of Hong Kong. When I visited the House of Commons in London earlier this year, I was practically strip-searched. One by one the newly-elected legislators came forward from their desks to take their oaths—no pledges of fealty to Queen Elizabeth II, just a simple promise to obey the law and serve the people of Hong Kong. Most spoke in Chinese, a few in English. Not a single white face was to be seen. I was tempted to call it the first all-Chinese Legco, then I remembered Ron Arculli, ethnically Indian. Gone are the members, such as the attorney general and the financial secretary, who used to sit in the assembly by virtue of the offices they held, like so many cabinet members on the government's front benches. In any case, all these high offices have been "localized", filled with ethnic Chinese people. Among the new members was Yeung Sum. In the end he had little trouble beating his challenger. As expected, the Democrats did well, winning fifteen of the twenty high-profile geographical constituencies. They and their allies among some of the smaller parties and independents will make up half of the new assembly. But the pro-Beijing crowd will be well-represented also. It may not have won some of the geographical districts, but managed to pick up seats from the more obscure functional constituencies.

Shortly after Legco was sworn in, I had breakfast with David Chu, who does not consider it an insult to be called the most pro-Beijing member of the legislature. A few days before we met, he introduced a motion prohibiting any private-member's bills that contravene the Sino-British agreements, and could not even get a seconder. That seemed to do nothing to dampen his ebullience, which he expresses in racing motorcycles and flying light airplanes. He and a British policeman, Angus Scott, set a record of a kind by paragliding from Hong Kong to Beijing in ten days. Chu worked for many years in the US and acquired US citizenship, which he later renounced, evidently fearing it would hamper a political career in Hong Kong after the handover.

I asked him if he thought China made any political blunders during the recent election.

"The biggest mistake was to take out advertisements in the Chinese-language press, urging people to vote for 'pro-Beijing' candidates. It offended a lot of people, who don't like being told who to vote for."

The other big mistake was publicly to remind everyone on the morning of polling day that it plans to dismantle the legislature on July 1, 1997. That statement must have come straight from Beijing since the pro-Beijing camp had asked the local Chinese representatives not to make any disastrous statements during the campaign—that is, to lie low.

We agreed that it was regrettable that [DAB chairman] Tsang Yok-sing lost his bid for a seat in Kowloon.

"The next time he runs, it will be after 1997, and probably under different rules, and people will say he couldn't win under a more democratic system."

"What kind of system would that be?" I asked.

"Oh, there are many ways to structure the electoral system. The most likely system for the first post-1997 election would be some kind of proportional system that would give pro-Beijing candidates a better chance."

# January 1996

*"We felt the collection was not appropriate in a modern Asian setting."*

NINETEEN NINETY-SIX—the Year of the Rat. From Hong Kong Island, it seems like mainland China is moving perceptibly closer. On either side of the Kowloon peninsula vast stretches of sand reach out into the water like oil slicks. To the east and west of the Star Ferry, the harbor is being altered beyond recognition. No, the Chinese are not making a premature grab for territory. Hong Kong is simply in the middle of a massive reclamation project. The current plans—which, of course, straddle 1997—call for filling in some five square miles of the inner harbor. From the coffee shop of the American Club at the top of Exchange Square, the newly reclaimed land being built for the new Outlying Islands Ferry Terminal already looks like it stretches halfway to Kowloon.

Land reclamation is an old story in Hong Kong, of course, as it is in many other cities with a waterfront and a need to accommodate an expanding population. Colonial governors began filling in the coastline as early as 1852, nine years after Hong Kong was founded, and many of the imposing buildings that make up the famous skyline rest on it. Hong Kong under the colonial regime has been a kind of engineers' paradise. Huge projects like this one are conceived in the bowels of government agencies, percolate upward, signed off by senior civil servants and the governor, then built. And if the project should cut off somebody's view, plow through a Song dynasty burial ground or disturb the habitat of a rare breed of mud slug, that's too bad.

That this project has aroused some active and vocal opposition is a sign of a new democratic spirit sweeping through the territory. Questions are being raised about it in Legco. Some talk circulates

of a private member's bill to curtail the government's ability to
reclaim more land from the waters without holding public hear-
ings. No doubt, this is one that the governor will find "not in the
best interests of Hong Kong" and veto if it should actually pass.
After all, any reclaimed land belongs to the crown; the government
makes a fortune from the long-term leases it sells from new land.
A developer paid about US$600 million for the first tract of new
land off Hunghom on the Kowloon peninsula. Workers are also
busy filling in the small naval basin at HMS *Tamar*. The anchorage
was moved several years ago to Stonecutters Island, on Kowloon
side, ostensibly to free valuable land near Central for development,
but also, it is said, to prevent the People's Liberation Army from
docking its frigates and patrol boats so visibly close to the sacred
precincts of commerce.

The Chinese are not very happy with this reclamation project,
since it involves a massive reshaping of the territory without their
approval. No doubt they also see it as another way for the British
to milk their last colony of lucrative engineering contracts in their
final year of administration. Beijing raised a huge outcry when
Hong Kong proceeded to build a new airport without consulting
with it first. Beijing became involved because the financing would
incur debts stretching well beyond 1997. Since reclamation is being
paid for through current revenues, Beijing has no such hook in
which to show its displeasure. But the signals are pretty clear that
there will be a re-evaluation later. By then, of course, half of the
project will be completed or irreversible. It is, after all, a lot easier
to dump dirt into the harbor than to scoop it out.

The hottest political topic these days is who will become Hong
Kong's first Chinese chief executive, replacing the British governor.
In January, liberal legislator Emily Lau introduced a motion in
Legco calling for the new chief to be elected by all of Hong Kong's
people, and it garnered a surprising amount of support. Council
president Andrew Wong had to cast the tie-breaking vote against
it. In fact, the choice will be made by a 400-member "Selection

Committee", a kind of electoral college yet to be named. Most people here realistically assume that the selection committee's deliberations will be a formality, and that the final decision will be made at the highest levels in Beijing. Indeed, it seems inconceivable that anybody would be chosen who is unacceptable to the Chinese leadership. The newspapers constantly speculate on who is in favor and who is not, who is on this "short list" and who is not. Last year when Chief Secretary Anson Chan's star seemed on the rise, much was made of her grandfather, Fang Zhenwu, a general who fought the Japanese in the 1930s and thus is considered a patriot despite having served on the Nationalist side. She paid a highly publicized visit to the family's ancestral home in Anhui province in August, lunching with the governor and visiting the general's old home. It all seemed orchestrated to demonstrate her "Chineseness" even though she has, in fact, been a servant of the British colonial administration for more than 30 years.

But after New Year, Chan's star seemed to dim, and a new favorite, shipping magnate Tung Chee-hwa emerged as the front-runner. In December, China's Hong Kong affairs chief Lu Ping seemed to dampen the Anson speculation deliberately by speaking cryptically about a "dark horse" emerging. As if on cue, the local Chinese press suddenly began running stories about Tung, stressing his apparent acceptability to the communist leaders in Beijing. Much is made of his common Shanghai origin with China's President Jiang Zemin and his closest advisers. It was reported that they chatted amiably in Shanghainese when they met in December in Shenzhen, while Jiang was showing off the special economic zone to visiting Cuban President Fidel Castro. Tung's brother-in-law, who runs the family business operations in Taiwan, is a director of the semi-official Cross-Strait Foundation and is a vocal critic of the man China hates most, Taiwan's President Lee Teng-hui. That can't hurt him in the eyes of the communist leader.

Significantly, Tung has the backing of Hong Kong's richest tycoon, billionaire Li Ka-shing. When Wheelock group chairman Peter Woo was subtly campaigning for the job a year ago, Li publicly stated that he didn't think it proper for the chief executive to come from local business ranks. Otherwise, there might be a conflict of interest and Hong Kong's image might suffer. This may have contributed to the short-lived boom for civil servants like Anson Chan and Sir Ti Liang Yang, the chief justice of the Supreme Court, or ex-senior civil servant, John Chan. But the billionaire reversed himself later by suggesting that Tung would be a good choice. And about the same time, China's Premier Li Peng dropped his opposition to having a local businessman take on the top post.

Tung's candidacy got another public boost when "old China friend", tycoon Henry Fok, came out vocally in his support. The two go back a long way. When the Tung family's shipping company, Orient Overseas International, was in financial trouble in the late 1970s shortly after Tung took over from his father, Fok engineered a large and timely loan that helped the company get its bearings. Fok has excellent and long-time connections in Beijing, serves as a vice chairman of the Chinese People's Political Consultative Conference, is close to ex-president Yang Shangkun and is said to have the ready ear of both Deng and Jiang. But the clearest signal came on January 26 when the 150 members of the new Preparatory Committee gathered in the Great Hall of the People in Beijing to receive their certificates of office from President Jiang. (As expected, no members of the Democratic Party were named to serve on the committee. That prompted Chris Patten to remark, "How can you justify trying to lock out those who, according to the [election] polls, represent 60 to 70 percent of the people of Hong Kong?")

The president seemed to go out of his way to find Tung in the crowd, a Preparatory Committee vice chairman, and shake his hand. In this way he sends a clear and unmistakable signal: this is my man.

But there are also signs that Beijing doesn't want the selection of the first chief to look too much like it was fixed even before the selection committee was chosen. Almost as soon as Fok announced his backing for Tung, another tycoon with equally impeccable connections across the border, Ann Tse-kai, plumped for property magnate Leung Chun-ying (who promptly disavowed any immediate interest in the post). At 42, Leung would seem a little young, and it may be that his name is being floated only as a possible future chief. Perhaps, too, he is a stalking horse for another figure who will emerge later, showing that the establishment is not entirely unified behind Tung. Or, it may be that the old friends are doing Beijing a favor by providing the show of a credible race for the job of chief executive.

When Lady Lydia Dunn announced late in 1995 that she was leaving Hong Kong for good to live permanently in Britain (where she has a townhouse in Kensington, a country estate in Gloucestershire and a seat in the House of Lords), it was almost as if somebody had spiked the Noon-Day Gun. (The Noon-Day Gun is an old naval cannon owned by Jardines that sits in front of the harbor, booming out the arrival of noon every day. From time to time celebrities leaving the colony, like Lady Dunn, are allowed the privilege of pulling the lanyard.) For years the elegant senior board member at Swire Pacific—and numerous other boards—was not only the most powerful woman in Hong Kong but almost the epitome of the old business establishment. Naturally, she proclaimed full and undying confidence in Hong Kong's future. Nevertheless, her departure this year is symbolic that power is fading from the old Anglo-Chinese élite to a more eclectic establishment and to new players, known as "red chips", which are Chinese-owned enterprises listed on the Hong Kong Stock Exchange.

At Hutchison Whampoa, which was the first *hong*, as the old line British trading companies are known, to come under full Chinese ownership when Li Ka-shing bought control, British managing director, Simon Murray, gracefully gave way to Canning Fok. Inchcape brought in Paul Cheng to fly the local flag, while Hongkong Telecom replaced the late Michael Gale with Linus Cheung. Even the Royal Hong Kong Jockey Club announced that a Chinese, Lawrence Wong, will become the club's next chief steward this year. How long, one has to wonder, will the Hongkong and Shanghai Banking Corporation keep a British expatriate as its chairman? Will John Gray still be in charge after 1997? It seems doubtful.

In other ways, large and small, the *hong*s are making the necessary adjustments. The Hongkong Bank has been conducting a "colonial audit" of its extensive collection of Chinese export trade art, replacing older paintings with works by contemporary Hong Kong artists. "We felt that the collection was not appropriate in a modern Asian setting," a bank's spokeswoman, Pamela George, told me. Yes, perhaps scenes of plump opium traders being carried around on sedan chairs are not exactly the kinds of images that companies interested in the "China play" would like to convey. Presumably the old pictures will wind up nostalgically on the walls of its new London holding company.

Like half of the companies listed on the Hong Kong Stock Exchange, the Hongkong Bank has taken the precaution of moving its nameplate abroad. In 1992, the bank bought the Midland, one of Britain's four clearing banks and turned itself into something called HSBC Holdings, headquartered in London. But the bank has also been careful to emphasize its deep roots in China, rediscovering the "Shanghai" in its name and even making efforts to recover its old headquarters on the famous Bund from communist sequestration. It was as if to say, "We are the Hong Kong and *Shanghai* Banking Corporation. We are patriotic too." But it is still doubtful whether China will want to permit "The Bank", as it is called, to maintain its commanding position after 1997. The Bank of China, whose gleaming new headquarters dominates the skyline, may come to dominate commerce as well. For the past few years it has been issuing about a fifth of the territory's bank notes. "Bit by bit, the Bank of China will move into a more dominant position, and the Hongkong Bank will give way gracefully," says Jimmy McGregor, who used to hold the General Chamber of Commerce seat in Legco and is now an executive councillor.

Looking back over the past ten years, the *hongs'* contribution to the economy of Hong Kong has increased in absolute terms with the general expansion of the colony's economy, but the proportion has decreased because the world has poured into the territory to take advantage of the business opportunities in China. That influx includes other British-owned concerns, such as the department-store chain of Marks & Spencer, which has no historical associations with Hong Kong and expects to compete on an equal footing with the other multinational companies that have set down roots without any special privileges.

History seems to weigh more heavily on that other pillar of the British colonial establishment, Jardine Matheson & Co. Of course, it carries a lot of baggage. "Jardines lives with an unfortunate past," says McGregor, referring to the company's history as an opium trader and a prime instigator of the 19th-century Opium War against China. "It has become a soft punching bag for Beijing, which feels it has to expiate old sins." Jardines didn't win any plaudits from the mainland when it moved its legal domicile to Bermuda in 1984, the same year that the Joint Declaration was signed, then followed up a decade later by completely delisting its shares from the Hong Kong Stock Exchange and shifting them to Singapore. The Keswick family resides in London and publicly endorsed Chris Patten's electoral reforms when every other *hong*, mindful of Beijing's strong opposition, remained prudently silent.

But Jardines, too, may be trying to repair its relations with Beijing. A year ago the new *taipan*, Alasdair Morrison, publicly apologized for his company's relocation moves. Lu Ping invited them to come back, "if they find that Singapore isn't as good as Hong Kong." Indeed, Jardines' shares have languished ever since they were shifted there. But the biggest sign that Jardines might be back in favor came in January when Beijing dropped its two-year opposition to the massive new container terminal project, delayed because two of the four berths had been allocated to Jardines. It would appear that the Noon-Day Gun will continue to resound across the harbor for a long time.

At last Beijing ended speculation on who will be the People's Liberation Army's big gun in Hong Kong after 1997. On January 28—592 days before the handover by the countdown clock in the lobby of the main barracks in Shenzhen—Major-General Liu Zhenwu was introduced as the commander of the troops that will march across the border at Lo Wu on July 1, and raise the five-star flag over Hong Kong as the territorial garrison. At 42, General Liu is obviously one of the Chinese army's up-and-comers, as is his designated deputy. Suave, English-speaking Senior Colonel Zhou Borong is a graduate of the British War College and is well-known and apparently well-liked on the military attaché circuit.

Most people here await the coming of the PLA with considerable trepidation. The vision of the bloody crackdown at Tiananmen Square in June 1989 is still fresh. Older residents have memories of how the PLA marched into Shanghai in 1949 to impose martial law. So Beijing is putting on a public relations campaign to convince everyone that the troops will be well-behaved. The soldiers, airmen and sailors have all been "hand-picked", we are told. *The Peoples' Daily* even ran a story about one Private Niu, a 19-year old soldier from Anhui province who is supposed to be the model soldier for Hong Kong. Not only does he speak English and Cantonese, but he is a prize-winning essayist. Unfortunately, when the journalists were allowed to inspect the garrison at its barracks in late January, this paragon could not be found. Nor were many other linguists or essayists evident among the troops, although they did display impressive skills in *kung fu* and the use of the bayonet.

Many of us unenlightened expatriates wondered just how demonstrations of prowess in bayonet thrusting were supposed to engender confidence. But people who watch Chinese television may have received a different, more positive message. Hong Kong reporters sought out neighbors, shopkeepers and other civilians living near the bases for interviews. They all testified how glad they were to have the soldiers around because it made them feel safer. Hong Kong newspapers often run stories of corruption, smuggling and highway robbery supposedly perpetrated by rogue PLA units, so this was perhaps a relief.

Everyone agreed that the élite Red First Regiment had a proud history, although the Hong Kong reporters didn't seem to be clear exactly what that history was. Did the regiment descend from the heroes of the Dadu River in the Long March, or did it trace its pedigree to the Autumn Harvest Uprising, Mao Zedong's attempt to incite a peasant revolt in 1927? Well, Chinese revolutionary history was never very strong on the colonial curriculum.

General Liu said that the PLA garrison in Hong Kong would not exceed the size of the current British forces, which numbered about nearly 10,000 troops in 1994 and now are reduced to only about 3,000 servicemen. Britain has been winding down its military establishment over the years (the British might bring one battalion back just before the handover so that it can formally march out again). The last regular unit of the British Army pulled out a couple of years ago. All that remains is a battalion of Gurkhas and a handful of Royal Navy patrol boats. Until they recently handed duties over to the police, their main mission was guarding against illegal aliens. In recent years there has been a deliberate effort to demilitarize many of the British garrison's duties, presumably so that the PLA troops will have as little to do as possible. Even such seemingly innocuous tasks as air-sea rescue have been given over to the marine police and the new Government Flying Service (which replaces the semi-military Royal Hong Kong Auxiliary Air Force).

The PLA's mission presumably is to assert Chinese sovereignty over the colony. Of course, it is also ideally located for possible operations in the South China Sea, where Beijing has claims disputed by other countries. Perhaps another unstated mission is simply to occupy and thus lay claim to some of the most valuable real estate in the colony. The British army, after all, got here first and claimed some of the best sites. All of Queensway near the naval basin, for example, was part of the military estate until 20 years ago. In 1994 prices, the military real estate was valued at about US$8 billion.

Another mission conceivably could be helping to maintain public order, if requested by the new SAR government. It is this, of course, that worries the locals the most. To help allay those fears President Jiang recently admonished army leaders to remember that their mission isn't to "liberate" Hong Kong. "Hong Kong will be run by Hong Kong people, and the PLA garrison should understand this fully," he said. Probably the territory's attitude can best be summed up as: out-of-sight, out of mind. So, many Hong Kong people were happy to hear that the troops would be mostly confined to their bases and probably allowed to venture into the capitalist enclave only in bunches under close supervision, like guided tour groups. In fact Private Niu is paid only about US$5 a month, roughly the cost of one beer in a Wan Chai bar, so duty here does not hold out the prospect for much fun. General Liu, himself, who is presumably the highest paid soldier, earns less than a third of the minimum wage for a housemaid. Some legislators are talking about ways Hong Kong might augment the pittance soldiers now get. Call it luxury pay?

At least none of them, including General Liu, will have to pay Hong Kong's salaries tax. I'm preparing mine, as news reports tell me that tax reform has become one of the important issues of the day back in the US. The authorities levy what is, for all practical purposes, a flat rate on income, with few deductions. As proponents of the flat tax back home never cease reminding, it is easy, if not exactly painless, to pay. All I'm doing is writing a check to the Inland Revenue. It is a rather large one. Hong Kong has a reputation for low taxes, and the maximum rate of 15 percent is certainly low compared with the 39 percent that Americans in the upper brackets pay. But it doesn't seem all that low when the tax is presented as a single, lump-sum demand note payable in cash. Hong Kong has no withholding, so it places a premium on being frugal, far-sighted and prudent in putting a little aside each month.

Since Hong Kong people are in the main no more frugal or far-sighted than anyone else, the banks do a big business in tax loans.

Hong Kong does not tax investment income or capital gains, and it has no deductions for home mortgage interest payments. That doesn't seem to have dampened enthusiasm for speculation in the property market. A few years ago—when apartments were being bought and sold a half-a-dozen times and at ever higher prices before they were even occupied—many in the territory began to wonder whether a capital gains tax might not have a salutary effect. Social welfare services don't depend much on charitable deductions either. Better to put one's faith in greed and horses. This year the Royal Hong Kong Jockey Club, the largest cash generator in the territory after the government, will spend millions of its betting earnings on new schools, hospitals, parks and other social amenities, which might otherwise have to be accommodated in the budget.

The Hong Kong model is often held up as a reason for its healthy investment climate, expanding economy and low unemployment rate. Maybe so, but it is difficult to imagine that a tax system that serves the needs of what is essentially a local government would work for a continental nation with world-wide responsibilities. After all, this territory has no army, sends no peacekeepers to Bosnia or anywhere else (though it did pay the considerable costs of maintaining refugee camps for Vietnamese boat people for many years), pays no real welfare or unemployment benefits and spurns old-age pensions. Economically if not politically integrated with its vast hinterland, Hong Kong earns large profits from business investments in China. But none of these profits is ever returned to China in the form of taxes. It is as if the people of New York City were never taxed to subsidize food for people of Appalachia or that the wealth earned in Toronto was never used to help boost incomes for fishermen in Newfoundland. The amazing thing is that Beijing has agreed to keep this system after 1997.

# March 1996 -457 DAYS

*"This rice is cooked."*

SURROUNDED BY TELEVISION NEWS cameramen and policemen, 61-year-old Indonesian-born Yau Sui-chun thrust her application at a weary immigration officer and declared her intention of becoming the last British subject in the last year of the last great colony of the empire. As a British Dependent Territory citizen, she will be eligible for a kind of ersatz British passport, good for travel abroad even after 1997. March 31, the last day for receiving applications, had turned into a stampede. Lines of people snaked their way all through Wan Chai, where the immigration offices are located. A stadium was converted into a kind of holding pen, and hundreds of hard-pressed immigration officers put in long hours of overtime processing the claims. By the witching hour, more than 54,000 Hong Kong people had applied to change their legal status in one day, 12,000 in the last few hours. The figure for the whole of 1995 was fewer than 35,000.

About three million Hong Kong people are already British dependent citizens by virtue of being born here. The rush was for people like Yau who have immigrated and must take out papers to get a British passport. Naturalization makes them eligible to obtain a British National Overseas (BNO) passport but does not make them citizens of the United Kingdom. A curious side agreement to the Joint Declaration in 1984—"taking into account the historical background of Hong Kong and its realities"—allows people born before July 1, 1997 to continue to travel on British documents, although they do not offer the holder the right to live permanently in Britain or obtain consular protection if they get in trouble abroad. The passports were, nevertheless, considered valuable by a population nervous about its prospects.

The Chinese government plans to issue a Hong Kong Special Administrative Region (SAR) passport, which will become valid on the turnover date and will be the only document that people born after 1997 can obtain. It is gaining international acceptance slowly. It was considered something of a concession when Prime Minister John Major, on a visit to the colony earlier this year, announced that Britain would allow SAR passport holders into the country without first having to obtain a visa. The BNO passport, on the other hand, permits visa-free entry into 81 countries (though not the US). Many countries worry that people using the SAR document will not be genuine Hong Kong travelers but mainlanders or well-connected Communist Party cadres, obtaining a document that offers more freedom of movement than the Chinese passport.

In Hong Kong, people, while obsessed with passports, are a little vague about their own nationality. Nowhere else in the world can so many recite in exhausting detail the minutiae of residency requirements in Canada, Australia or the US. People say in passing, "by the way, my husband's application has been approved. We leave in April when the weather in Toronto gets warmer" and everyone understands immediately that their Canadian citizenship has been approved. They like to boast about how much money they made selling their apartments in Hong Kong and how cheap those big houses in Vancouver are by local standards. But ask them their nationality, and they are stumped. Most people would probably mumble something like, "I'm from Hong Kong," or "I'm Chinese but from Hong Kong." Nobody would say they are British, even if they happened to hold a British document. Not even those people who have just sworn to "bear true allegiance to Her Majesty, Queen Elizabeth the Second, her heirs and successors" in order to become British Dependent Territory citizens.

Of course, the man in the passport line has precious little loyalty to the far-off monarch. Long ago, London made it exceedingly clear that hordes of Hong Kong refugees were not welcome in Britain before 1997, or anytime thereafter. In response, the Hong Kong man, seeking a place of refuge if things go wrong, has turned to more welcoming countries, Canada and Australia in particular, and to a lesser degree the United States. This has often meant spending several years and several cold winters in Toronto, or balmy ones in Vancouver, or long separations from wife and children as they move abroad establishing permanent residency while the breadwinner stays behind to earn money. The Chinese call these people "astronauts". This curious term is a pun on the Cantonese word for "spaceman", which can also be taken to mean "a man without his wife".

The average Hongkonger looks on this hard-earned passport mostly as a kind of travel insurance policy. He sees nothing inconsistent, for example, in traveling to China on Home Visit Permits issued by Beijing, even though these documents imply citizenship in China. Film director Michael Hui, a Canadian "passport holder", expressed the local ethic balder than most when he said, "If Tonga were to say I can get a passport, if I invest US$5,000 and stay a day, I would take it immediately. It's got nothing to do with patriotism—just traveling convenience."

About a million Hongkongers have obtained such travel insurance, either directly or through their relatives. So it is a matter of no small concern to many people in Hong Kong how Beijing treats migrants who have obtained the right to live abroad but who want to stay in the colony after 1997. China does not recognize dual citizenship, so strictly speaking, these people should be treated as foreigners, requiring that they obtain residency permits, give up the right to vote and become subject to deportation should they break the law. Unless, of course, they renounce their citizenship and reapply to become Chinese, which would mean canceling the insurance. During his visit to Hong Kong in April, Lu Ping, China's Hong Kong Affairs chief, gave a speech that seemed to reflect considerable pragmatism on the part of Beijing. China will assume that all emigrants living in or returning to Hong Kong after 1997 are Chinese citizens unless they specifically and publicly declare themselves to be foreign nationals. Presumably, this would take place at the immigration counter where, on returning,

Hongkongers have a choice of presenting either passport or iden-
tification card. If they keep silent about their foreign citizenship,
then China will disregard their foreign nationality and view their
passports as merely travel documents, which is how most people
view them anyway.

A more wrenching decision awaits the minority that wants to
remain active in Hong Kong's political affairs after 1997. Not a few
members of the current legislature are Australians, Canadians,
British or even Americans. Democratic legislator Huang Chen-ya
says he wants to keep his Australian passport after 1997 in order
not to become stateless. David Chu, on the other hand, renounced
his American citizenship a few years ago to further his political
ambitions. At the moment he travels on something called a Certificate of Identity and plans to obtain an SAR passport after the
turnover. Chu may have been unusual in renouncing his citizenship. Many in Hong Kong, who loudly proclaim their loyalty to
China and their undying confidence in the territory's future, have
taken out insurance papers or made sure that somebody in their
family has them. Prominent pro-Beijing politician Tsang Yok-sing
was embarrassed a few years ago during elections for local councils.
His party was loudly proclaiming its confidence in the future when
a Chinese-language newspaper revealed that he had applied for
Canadian citizenship shortly after the June 4, 1989 Tiananmen
massacre. Apparently, he later withdrew his application, but his
wife and daughter moved to Vancouver to establish residency,
while he stayed behind. So like many other Hongkongers, he too
has become an astronaut.

Those who stood for hours in the passport line, however, were
not the territory's power brokers. They were ordinary people—taxi
drivers, clerks, waiters. They don't hold British, Canadian or
American passports, nor do they have the means with which to
purchase citizenship in Tonga or some other country of convenience. They believe profoundly that they are Chinese, even as
they line up to get a kind of British citizenship. If questioned, most
would say something like, "It is handy to have just in case" or "It's

insurance". Yau Sui-chun told reporters she would probably apply for an SAR passport after 1997 in addition to her British document. And, of course, she also has her Indonesian passport. In the uncertain times to come, one can't have too many options.

HOPES DASHED AS DEMOCRATS BARRED FROM CONSULTATIONS
*—South China Morning Post*

Something like open warfare has broken out over the Preparatory Committee's decision March 23 to disband the legislature elected last September and replace it with a temporary appointed one, the so-called provisional legislature. Chris Patten, never one to mince words, called it "a black day for democracy in Hong Kong". He also noted the irony of the committee's voting to disband the elected legislature on the same day that Taiwan's people were re-electing President Lee Teng-hui in China's first free presidential election. The action was not unexpected, of course. Since 1994 when negotiations over electoral reforms broke down, Beijing has publicly been talking about building a "second stove", which is an expression for a complete parting of the ways, as in "We don't like what you're cooking, so we'll build our own stove and cook up our own recipe." In the Hong Kong context, that means creating in essence a parallel government, of which the most important element is the provisional legislature.

Still, the action rippled through this community like the swells of an approaching typhoon. It was accompanied by some heavy-handed treatment of the one member of the committee to vote against it, democratic legislator Frederick Fung. By this action, Fung may have disqualified himself from serving in the provisional legislature or on the body that will pick its members as well as the new chief executive. Then when Chief Secretary Anson Chan questioned the action in public, Chinese officials demanded that all top civil servants who wanted to keep their posts after 1997 pledge loyalty to the interim legislature. Beijing later backtracked, saying only that the bureaucrats should not go public with their opinions, but considerable damage was done to the territory's always shaky confidence.

Against this backdrop, China's point man on Hong Kong, Lu Ping, flew into town to preside over a series of meeting on the progress of the handover and the selection of people to serve on the electoral college that will elect the new governor. Though billed as "consultations" it was a curious kind of dialogue. From the moment he arrived at Kai Tak airport, Lu Ping was dogged by demonstrators. A couple of rubber tires were burned, leaving big, black smudges on the entrance driveway to the elegant Grand Hyatt Hotel, site of the consultation exercise. Bird cages were smashed. "We don't want to become canaries who only sing the song the master wants to hear," is how legislator Cheung Man-kwong explained the symbolism. Some students brandished caged turtles to symbolize the Chinese and their local backers who retreat into their shells rather than hear dissenting opinions. Not exactly like the streets of Seoul, but a ruder welcome than many of the Beijing delegates are probably used to seeing.

The Democrats were probably correct in thinking that political theater rather than dialogue would better advance their cause. Beijing, after all, has said that the provisional legislature is an accomplished fact, not a matter for further discussion. In a twist to the second stove phrase, Foreign Minister Qian Qichen told his British counterpart: "This rice is cooked." The party's leader, Martin Lee, left Hong Kong the same weekend for a lengthy lobbying trip to Canada and the US, intending "to tell it like it is," as he said before departing. He and his colleague Yeung Sum did the telling to Vice President Al Gore and the president's national security adviser, Anthony Lake. "Dismantling a democratically elected legislature and replacing it with a rubber stamp is a breach of the international treaty which the US government supported and applauded."

A few of the more liberal-minded members of the Preparatory Committee seem to have had at least a dim idea that the consult-ations had the making of a public relations disaster if dissenting opinions were excluded totally. So an invitation was extended to the Professional Teachers Union even though it meant a face-to-face encounter with its leaders Szeto Wah and Cheung Man-kwong. The two tough critics of Beijing are core leaders of the Alliance in Support of the Patriotic and Democratic Movement in China, which supported the students in Tiananmen Square in 1989. For that reason, Beijing considers them subversive and has refused to deal with them.

At the last moment, the PTU was disinvited, presumably because some members loudly denounced the provisional legislature even before Lu Ping had set foot in the colony. A substitute invitation to address the committee was extended to the Hong Kong Students Federation, whose members predictably did their best to get themselves evicted. As soon as they entered the meeting room, they shouted slogans and ripped off their jackets and displayed T-shirts with "raping public opinion" and "phony consultations" written on them. It was a chance for the Democrats to re-establish some kind of contact with China's representatives. But it didn't work, and another opportunity may not arise before the handover.

Patten was away in London during most of this tempest. It fell to Anson Chan to be Hong Kong's main point of contact. She held one highly publicized dinner meeting with Lu at Xinhua's guest house in Stanley, where China's representative made clear that senior civil servants who don't cooperate with the provisional legislature will be unable to serve in their current posts in the new administration. A few people in Hong Kong may still think Chan has a chance of becoming Hong Kong's first Chinese governor, but they must be dwindling rapidly. She may possibly continue as head of the 180,000-strong civil service after the handover, providing a badly-needed element of continuity. David Chu still thinks she has a chance, despite her open support of the governor's stand on maintaining the current legislature.

"Her duty is to go along with official policy. Nobody should hold it against a civil servant," he told me.

Public opinion polls also show that she is the most popular choice for the first chief. But she will have to back-pedal furiously, after the takeover, since she has made some rather strong statements. Come January, when the Queen's Honors List is published, it would not be surprising to see Mrs. Chan become Dame Anson Chan and thus fade away into honorable retirement.

Meanwhile, the governor rolled back into town in a fighting mood. Meeting with the legislature, he said the government would offer no help to the caretaker body.

"The provisional legislature has nothing to do with the government of Hong Kong between now and June 30, 1997," he said. He later told reporters, "we'll do nothing, that's spelled N-O-T-H-I-N-G, whatsoever to take away from, to undermine, the authority of Hong Kong's Legislative Council."

But the civil service is now backed into an uncomfortable position. It's hard to see how the issue can be finessed. Beijing had made it clear that the provisional legislature will be a working legislature.

"There are things that have to be done by the first second of July 1—for example, the confirmation of members of the new Court of Final Appeal," Chu said over breakfast one morning while we were discussing the latest events.

The caretaker body seems ready to legislate in three main areas. One will be to dismantle Patten's electoral reforms and write a new election law, one that is closer, they would argue, to Hong Kong's post-1997 constitution, the Basic Law. If the new legislature stuck primarily to this one task—simply dismantling the nine expanded constituencies that were the core of Patten's reforms, and then called for a new election—controversy might be limited.

Beijing, however, seems determined to do much more. It may want to use this temporary body of hand-picked and trusted supporters to overturn everything that the British have done here that Beijing doesn't like since the signing of the Joint Declaration in 1984. Already the Preparatory Committee has requested a list of all ordinances and regulations enacted in Hong Kong since that date. Beginning in 1991, Legco passed a Bill of Rights and began modifying several statutes which the colonial administration had been armed with over the years to deal with disturbances and public disorder. These included things like the power to censor newspapers and films, impose martial law or stop and search suspicious people. These laws are now routinely described as "draconian", though I can't remember much fuss being made over them in years past. The irony is that most of these laws, when they were used at all, were usually aimed at suppressing communists and other left-wing activists.

The committee has also made clear that it intends to scrutinize carefully and possibly modify the 1997/98 transitional budget, which is likely to put exceptional pressure on the financial secretary, Donald Tsang. How can he avoid cooperating with the provisional body and thus running foul of his boss? Another knighthood in the offing and an honorable exit? As for the remaining department heads, all have been invited to attend "get-acquainted" sessions with Xinhua, China's *de facto* consulate, which seem a lot more like job interviews. It's not hard to figure out what kinds of questions will be asked. No doubt high on the list: Will you support the provisional legislature? At least the venue, the plush Jockey Club in Happy Valley, is pleasant enough.

A pro-Beijing politician once told me that China's leaders have two overriding concerns in the final year of the transition. One is to try to win over the hearts and minds of Hong Kong's people. The second is foiling various British "plots". On recent evidence, it seems clear that goal number two has priority, even if it means undermining confidence in the territory's future. "There is a school of thought that Beijing can address the first goal after the British have left," he said.

No one should underestimate the depth of distrust that Beijing has always harbored toward Britain. In the conspiratorial mind of the elderly leaders, the biggest task that they and their friends in the territory have is to uncover the land mines that Britain has planted for them to step on after 1997 and defuse them one by one.

Hence, in China's mind, Patten's unilateral decision to expand the number of directly elected seats in the legislature is not a noble though tardy attempt to bring a measure of democracy to Hong Kong before Britain departs. It is a means of leaving in place a strong pro-British or at least pro-Western government (though one freely elected by a population overwhelmingly Chinese). The new Bill of Rights is not a way of bringing the territory's laws into conformance with international norms and boosting confidence but a way of "loosening the screws" just before the handover in order to make it harder for the new administration to govern. Proposals to increase spending on the territory's modest social welfare programs are seen as a selfish bid by the outgoing administration to curry warm feelings with the local population, while saddling the new government with crippling spending and debts.

Of course, the governor can be expected to defend the creation on which he has staked much of his reputation. But, unfortunately, he seems bent on polarizing the community around this one issue. Patten has always had a strong tendency to treat the Chinese leaders as if they were merely opposition shadow ministers and he was debating with them from the Treasury bench in the House of Commons. The edge of sarcasm has become even sharper of late. After Lu Ping spent a week dodging demonstrators, finally slinking away through an obscure border crossing, Patten rubbed more salt in the wound by loudly proclaiming that *he* never had to leave a Hong Kong function through the back door.

In January a team from the British Broadcasting Corporation (BBC) came to Hong Kong to prepare for what it believes will be one of the biggest stories of the decade. It surveyed hotels and accommodation (likely to be tight) and the logistics of exhaustive coverage of the historic event. More than 2,000 news people from 170 organizations have already told the Government Information Service that they intend to cover the handover ceremonies. However, the BBC team was unable to discover one critical fact to help in planning—exactly what was going to happen.

The usual script for this type of colonial transition—the one that has the governor, decked out in his ceremonial garb, and possibly one of the lesser members of the royal family standing side-by-side with the new nation's prime minister as the Union flag is slowly lowered, the new country's flag raised and the new national anthem was played for the first time—does not really apply in this case. After all, Britain is not preparing Hong Kong for independence but returning it to another country. Patten, who has never worn the traditional uniform anyway, is a pariah on the mainland. In the four years he has been here he has never met with any senior Chinese leader. China would prefer that he didn't attend any farewell ceremony at all. Yet it is inconceivable that the last governor would not have a role in the ending of Britain's last major colony.

As things stand now, there will probably be two essentially separate ceremonies. For the British, the big day will be June 30, the last of their 156-year administration. London hopes to turn it into something grand, possibly with the Prince of Wales officiating. The Chinese are in no mood to sit still and listen as the British recount their past glories. A cool toast, a brisk business-like handshake and the governor's quick exit would be to their liking.

"What is there to celebrate?" asks Tsang Yok-sing, noting that Hong Kong became British territory only after China's humiliating defeat in the Opium War.

"The British want a high-profile ceremony positive to the image of Britain. Well, they won't get it," said legislator David Chu.

For China the real celebration gets underway on July 1, the first full day of sovereignty. That day and the one following it have already been declared public holidays, and July 1 will remain Hong Kong's regular holiday to commemorate the event. This is the day that China's top leaders, among them President Jiang Zemin and Premier Li Peng, plan to fly in to preside over the inauguration of the new chief executive and the government of the Special Administrative Region. Many of the old revolutionaries say they can't die in peace until they have been able to witness the glorious event with their own eyes. Lu Ping has been trying to persuade them to stay at home and attend a separate function in the Great Hall of the People in Beijing.

China's leaders would like to attract many of the world's leaders to help them celebrate what they undoubtedly consider a historic righting of an ancient wrong. But as it will feature the installation of a new administration, including the controversial unelected provisional legislature, many leaders in the West may feel it is impolitic to attend. This will no doubt be seen, remembered and resented as another snub. Maybe the British should put the key under the doormat and just leave.

# May 1996

*"The dances will continue to be danced, and the horses will continue to race."*

THE PATRIARCH, DENG XIAOPING, always had shrewd insight into the local psyche. Horse racing is so much a part of Hong Kong's social fabric that it would be impossible to imagine life here without it. Every Wednesday the territory seems to comes to a halt. As night falls, thousands of fans clog the crowded roads leading to the huge stadium in Happy Valley. A roar from the crowd erupts as the horses leave the starting gates. Images of pounding flesh flicker across the huge outdoor television screen in the infield, placed so that the fans can see which horse is in the lead even as they are running on the far side of the track.

Away from the track, taxi drivers listen to the race on their radios while waiting for a fare and others huddle around the television monitors at the betting outlets. The privileged members of the Royal Hong Kong Jockey Club watch from their private boxes high above the track, studying their tip sheets on white-linen-clothed tables, while a waiter pours the third glass of wine. Just before the race begins, some stroll on to the balcony to watch through their field glasses, others stay behind to observe on television monitors. If the member happens to be an owner, and if the owner's horse comes in first, a mad dash follows down to the winner's circle to receive the silver trophy from the chief steward and pose for pictures, flanked by a bevy of beauty queens. The variety of bets and the potential winnings are staggering in their complexity. The uninitiated—faced with tierces, quinellas, perfectas—retreat to tried-and-true win, show and place. The record winning for a HK$10 (US$1.30) bet is more than US$1 million, won in 1995 on something called a "triple trio", one of the most complicated wagers in the world.

The British had hardly taken up residence before they laid out a makeshift horse track in Happy Valley on virtually the only stretch of flat land on Hong Kong Island. That was in 1846. By 1871, horse racing was sanctioned as the only legal form of betting in the colony, and in 1884 the club was formed. From the beginning, it was the focal point of colonial social life. It was often said that Hong Kong was run by the Royal Hong Kong Jockey Club, the Hongkong and Shanghai Banking Corporation, Jardine Matheson and the governor—in that order. Certainly there was no better sign that one had "arrived" than to be named one of the stewards, most of whom were leading members of the British *hong*s. Chinese were not allowed to join the club until 1923.

Today, of course, the twelve stewards are predominantly Chinese. In 1994 Alasdair Morrison, the *taipan* of Jardines, failed to win appointment to the stewards. Instead of going to the "princely *hong*", one of the "red princes", Larry Yung, chief of CITIC Pacific, an investment arm of the Chinese government, was drafted into serving. But nothing was more emblematic of the changes taking place than the appointment of Lawrence Wong as the club's first Chinese chief steward, a post usually held by retired British army generals. Wong took on his new duties in April, moving from Taiwan, where he was the chief executive officer of Ford Lio Ho Motor Co., the joint venture with the American car maker. He cheerfully acknowledged that he didn't know anything about bloodlines, but he could read the bottom line, which might prove even more useful. In his first meeting with the racing press, the former Taiwan Businessman of the Year studded his conversation with terms such as "economies of scale" and "product management". Racing, he repeatedly said, was "our product", the punters presumably the "customers".

Well, why not? The jockey club is more than just a sporting establishment and social club. It is a major industry, one of the largest in Hong Kong, with a turnover annually approaching US$10 billion. The profits beyond expenses are plowed into charitable works, such as schools, clinics, even the building of Hong Kong's third university. All of this, we're told, helps to keep taxes low. Indeed, Wong's training in engineering is probably more useful than a deep knowledge of horseflesh. The club is moving into electronic "telebetting" in a big way. It simulcasts races now to Canada, Australia, the US, all places with large Hong Kong immigrant populations unwilling to forego totally their favorite pastime. The club is said to be one of the world's leading companies in developing secure software, complete with stored-value cards and PIN codes.

The club's position after 1997 seems safe even though racing's legal position in China is somewhat ambiguous. The communists banned all forms of gambling as bourgeois after they took over in 1949. Nevertheless, race tracks have sprung up in some of the larger cities. The Guangzhou Jockey Club across the border attracts between 30,000 and 40,000 punters to its Thursday races, about as many as attend the average meet in Hong Kong. Of course, if one were rude enough to point to the hundreds of people approaching the ticket windows clutching ten-yuan notes in their hands and ask whether gambling occurs on the premises, the club officials would no doubt be "shocked". The Hong Kong Jockey Club is shrewdly helping Chinese equestrian authorities rebuild the racing industry there by sending horses and trainers to Shanghai and other Chinese cities with racing tracks. It remains to be seen whether such races as the Queen Elizabeth II Cup become the Deng Derby. What does Wong think about July 1, 1997? It's just another day at the races.

The jockey club voted to drop the "Royal" from its title effective this July without much fuss. But over at Kellett Island, the members of the Royal Hong Kong Yacht Club were not about to give up without a struggle the title granted them by Queen Victoria in 1895. At two extraordinary general meetings the weekend sailors wrestled with the question: Should they preserve the title and the traditions that go with it? Or, should they decide that staying royal is an expensive anachronism when the territory is passing under new management?

What to do with the "R-word" may not be the biggest of Hong Kong's worries as it hurtles toward July 1, 1997, but it can still be emotionally wrenching. At the stroke of midnight, the Union Jack will be hauled down for the last time. Other symbols of royalty such as portraits of Queen Elizabeth II (most of them looking like they have been hanging there since Coronation Day, 1953) will be taken down in post offices and other government offices. Public institutions such as the Royal Hong Kong Police and the Royal Observatory will remove their imperial prefixes as a matter of course on the transition day. The soon-to-be-just-plain Hong Kong Police are already designing a new cap badge that replaces the crown and sailing junk with the official flower and a modern Hong Kong skyline. But nothing in the Basic Law obliges private institutions to conform. So, one by one, they have to decide whether to maintain the tradition or bow to the reality that Hong Kong is becoming a part of a country that still nurses resentments over its treatment by European imperialists.

"We have members who serve on Beijing-appointed committees, and they tell us that we can keep the word royal in our title, but that we would be wise to drop it," said Tony Scott, the commodore of the yacht club, when I asked him why he wanted to drop the prefix.

"Anyone not listening to that advice would be in denial. It would be hard to ask the new chief executive to be a club patron if we insist on keeping the royal. We also call on the navy for help in many of our races. How can we say to the new senior naval officer, 'We're a royal club, but can we still get your help, please?' "

A significant minority, however, seems prepared to put tradition ahead of prudence. When the name change came to a vote at an emotional meeting in November, it failed to get the needed 75 percent approval by two votes. "I think that surrendering the title is not the way to go," said Ian Dubin, a Canadian royalist, who led the fight to preserve the title in the name. He and his colleagues argued that dropping the royal amounted to kowtowing. More than 600 members attended a second meeting at the club on May 20. Although 60 percent voted to drop the title, it was not enough under the three-quarters majority rule. A resigned Scott said he would drop the matter for a while. "We still have 400 days to go."

That other social bastion of colonialism, the Royal Hong Kong Golf Club, voted to drop its prefix earlier in May. Said club captain Ron Carstairs, "It's in our interest to move forward." The RSPCA is to become just plain SPCA in January. But the Royal Asiatic Society said it plans to keep the title. "Even our Chinese members think it lends us a certain cachet," said president David Gilkes.

\*    \*    \*    \*

"A Rubicon has been crossed in relations between the Governor, Chris Patten, and the business community," thundered the *South China Morning Post* soon after the governor returned in early May from a lobbying trip to the United States. "The ground is shifting in a radical fashion." The cause for this apparent movement in tectonic plates was a cover story in the international edition of *Newsweek,* which also carried an interview with the governor. Under the headline BETRAYING HONG KONG, the writer rather bluntly accused Hong Kong's business establishment of selling Hong Kong down the river. "The tycoons gained the most from a free-wheeling society, so why are they working with China to impose communist-style controls?" In a separate interview Patten also appeared to take the businessmen to task: "Why is it that privileged people are prepared to sign up to arrangements whose sole intention is to choke off the voice of those who by every measure represent the majority of public opinion? Well, I'll say this: They wouldn't be doing it if most of them didn't have foreign passports in their back pockets."

Seven business organizations, headed by the Hong Kong General Chamber of Commerce, hit back in a letter to Prime Minister John Major, which was also published as a quarter-page advertisement in the *Post:* "Whatever the precise words the governor may or may not have used, we very much regret that he has given the impression that business people in Hong Kong do not have the territory's best interest at heart. In doing so, he has cast doubt on the integrity of the business community and undermined the tremendous contribution business has made to the development of Hong Kong. . . ." and a lot more in that vein. Major responded with a defense of his friend and former colleague, pointing out that Patten had merely tried to answer the skeptical questions which had been triggered by recent unsettling moves and statements coming out of Beijing that have damaged confidence in Hong Kong. "The governor has been doing his best to put things right. It would be helpful if, when statements are made threatening Hong Kong's legislature, its Bill of Rights, the independence of the judiciary and the political neutrality of the civil service, the leadership of your chambers could make its voices heard on those issues too."

So what to make of this latest storm? *Newsweek*'s gloomy assessment of Hong Kong's future after the British depart is fairly characteristic of the line now being taken by most of the Western press. It harks back at least to *Fortune*'s cover story of June, 1995, "The Death of Hong Kong". Certainly the tenor of most of the editorials written in the *Asian Wall Street Journal* has been down-beat. When a few weeks back the Hong Kong Trade Development Council held a rather innocuous seminar touting the good things that it says will continue to happen in Hong Kong after 1997, and after it invited Lu Ping, then in town, as a guest speaker, Philip Bowring wrote in the *International Herald Tribune* that the group was "evolving into another mouth-piece for 'patriotic' pronouncements." He dismissed the provisional legislature as a "quisling" legislature. Wonder what term he would use to describe all of the Chinese who have served the British colonial masters over the years?

In fact, Patten's remarks in *Newsweek* were fairly tame compared with some of the things he's been saying of late. Three months ago he lamented China's habit of talking only to "billionaires whose principal concern is that they should go on being billionaires." In February, the *Daily Telegraph* reported that Patten had accused tycoons of wanting only to keep the good life going for themselves. He has said similar things in the Chinese-language media, as well. But his interview appeared in a prestigious American news magazine, not some Chinese language daily, and it followed the governor's high-profile trip to the US, which, in turn, had followed the equally high profile trip by Martin Lee and his fellow Democrats. Perhaps there was more than a little pique that business leaders who later visited the US under the auspices of the new mouthpiece of conservative businessmen, the Better Hong Kong Foundation, did not get nearly as much attention.

The truth is Patten has never been a favorite of the business community. Nor have most of the business tycoons been very supportive of him or his program. Of all the major business leaders in Hong Kong, only the Keswick brothers, who own a controlling interest in Jardines, openly endorsed the political reforms and supported Patten. Everyone else kept silent. Most of the tycoons have never favored expanding democracy here. They figure that it will only bring into office a lot of politicians who will try to curry favor with the voters by creating more public old age pensions or other public services that might raise taxes. Strangely, that is almost exactly the same position of the communists in China. And, they argue, why jeopardize their growing contacts with the future sovereign to champion Patten's reforms? They never supported them in the first place.

*       *       *       *

The hallways of the Pui Kiu Middle School on Hong Kong Island echo with the bustle of students changing classes, all of them dressed in neat blue and gray uniforms. It is a normal scene at any of the colony's better-off fee-charging schools. The only thing out of the ordinary is the display of old black-and-white photographs on the wall of the student union building. They commemorate the

May 4 Movement of 1919, one of the turning points of modern Chinese history.

"There is not much difference between our school and government schools, but here the students are freer to talk about their own country," Vice Principal Anna Yip told me as she took me on a tour.

The country she is referring to is, of course, China, not Britain.

Since the founding of the People's Republic in 1949, a small but close-knit "patriotic" or pro-Beijing community has existed in Hong Kong. It had its own schools, newspapers, even department stores. Many of the members were families of Chinese people sent to work for Xinhua, the Bank of China, or some of the other mainland establishments here. With the handover just a year away, this community is beginning to become a part of the mainstream.

The principal of Pui Kiu, Tsang Yok-sing, has emerged as one of the leading pro-Beijing political figures in Hong Kong. He is often the media's first choice in seeking sound-bites on China's position on this or that after July 1, 1997; his opinion pieces appear frequently in the mainstream press. These days, he is more likely to be found at the headquarters of the Democratic Alliance for the Betterment of Hong Kong, the leading pro-Beijing party that he chairs. So it was there, in his modern but rather small and spartan office with a window overlooking an alley, rather than a panoramic view of the harbor, that I went to meet him.

I wanted to talk less about the politics of the day and more about his own political evolution. He does not come from one of the traditional leftist families, such as sons and daughters of the Bank of China employees. His father was a civil servant. He and his brother were educated, not at one of the left-wing schools but at Saint Paul's College, no doubt at some sacrifice by his parents. Later, he was a prize mathematics student at Hong Kong University. But rather than follow the capitalist road of other rags-to-riches tycoons in the territory, he took a revolutionary turn.

The seminal event in his formative years was the arrest of his younger brother, Tak-sing, for distributing a pamphlet in the school yard criticizing the way Chinese history was being taught in the colonial schools—an episode his brother often mentions when the subject turns to freedom of the press post-1997. Tak-sing later said that, "my political development had very little to do with growing up with Marx and Engels and a lot to do with growing up as Chinese man in a British colony." At age seventeen he was sentenced to two years in Stanley prison. He is now editor of the *Ta Kung Po,* one of the two leftist newspapers in Hong Kong.

One of Tsang Yok-sing's favorite topics in newspaper opinion columns is the way history was taught, or not taught, in the British schools when he was growing up. "In the 1960s most history [of China] stopped at the Opium War, and all of the instruction was in English," he recalls. "Even now history is still an elective, and many young people don't take it after age fifteen."

"All talk of politics was more or less taboo," he recalled. "We had some 'civics' lessons, in which we learned how the post office worked or how to be law-abiding. But I can't put the blame all on the British. The fact is, for a few decades after World War II, politics was a very sensitive subject. It meant being either pro-Kuomintang or pro-Communist. Most people simply wanted to have nothing to do with either."

By the end of the 1960s, there were about a dozen pro-China schools. "If you were patriotic, you supported these schools, read the pro-China newspapers and bought your shirts at China Products." Despite the chaos across the border, many people who came of age in the 1960s sometimes look back on that time as a kind of golden age. By the end of the decade about a dozen left-wing schools were scattered around Hong Kong.

They were left pretty much alone by the authorities, although Tsang remembers some harassment from the British authorities.

"All of the schools were inspected. I remember hiding some proscribed books, such as the works of Mao Zedong. A few teachers and principals were deported during those years."

"We benefited from the Cultural Revolution, and the spillover of ideological fervor," he said. His own school expanded to four branches and 4,000 students; now there is only one branch.

A drastic change followed the Cultural Revolution. Pragmatism was the order of the day. "People said even Deng Xiaoping sends his children abroad for schooling, why should we support the pro-Beijing schools? We survived mainly because of the continuing support from past students." Many closed for lack of patronage.

During the 1970s the Hong Kong government began pouring money into all kinds of social welfare programs, including education, establishing the territory's first free schools and subsidizing many private ones, though for political reasons the left-wing schools like Pui Kiu were not included. Meanwhile, the economy had begun its take off, costs were rising, it became difficult to recruit and hold teachers.

Since the signing of the Joint Declaration in 1984, things have improved significantly. Differences between the various schools, Christian, government and private, have narrowed. Chinese history is now taught in all schools up to the era of the Cultural Revolution, although modern subjects can still be sensitive. The terms "Republic of China" and "country" in reference to Taiwan are being expunged from school textbooks after next year's handover in deference to Beijing's One-China policy. How to present the Tiananmen massacre of June 4, 1989 continues to be a difficult subject, too. In 1994, the secretary for education, Dominic Wong, was criticized when he urged the omission from history texts of any mention of the incident. But politics is no longer strictly taboo. Posters of the Basic Law are often displayed. Tsang himself is a welcome lecturer even at government-funded or Christian schools. The Pui Kiu is now offered a government subsidy as are other private schools.

"In the past ten years, the differences between the left-wing and other schools has narrowed. We're teaching more or less the same things."

Does that mean that schools like Pui Kiu have lost their reason for being, I asked?

"We have got to think hard what kind of a role we'll play after 1997," Tsang mused. "Are we to become just like any other school in Hong Kong? We had a clear mission in the 1950s and 60s. We felt a need to teach another generation to know and love their country. Now perhaps we have another mission in preparing students for the return to China.

"Today almost the only thing that distinguishes Pui Kiu from any other school in Hong Kong is the fact that we honor China's National Day on October 1. No government school in Hong Kong does that."

Then a mischievous smile seems to flit across his face.

"At least not yet."

# June 1996

*"The churches have never experienced so many heavy issues."*

THE INFORMATION OFFICES of the Alliance in Support of the Patriotic and Democratic Movement in China are located in a dingy building on Portland Street in a crowded part of Kowloon better known for *karaoke* lounges and brothels. It occupies two rooms piled with boxes of political tracts and plastic statues of the Goddess of Democracy, the symbol of the democracy movement in China which vaguely resembles the Statue of Liberty. It would have been hard to find the place if I had not been taken there by Leung Kwok-hung after our rendezvous at the Mongkok subway station. Fortunately, he was easy to spot in the crowd, his long black ponytail and jeans making him look like an American Indian or a sixties-era rebel, which, in a way, is what he is.

I last had a fleeting glimpse of Leung on television as he set fire to a box of tires on the driveway of the Grand Hyatt Hotel, protesting the Preparatory Committee's decision to disband the elected Legco, announced during Lu Ping's visit last April. He is often seen at the head of demonstrations outside the legislature or leading a sit-in in front of Xinhua's headquarters in Happy Valley. If anyone is marked down in some black book for arrest after 1997, it would be he. Some say that the Chinese dislike him more than any of Hong Kong's better-known democracy advocates, such as Martin Lee or Alliance leader Szeto Wah.

They make a nice study in contrast—Lee and Leung. Martin Lee is a wealthy barrister, well-spoken in a clipped British manner and always well-dressed. When he goes abroad, he is received by people like Vice President Al Gore or Republican leader Bob Dole. Leung scrapes out a living by working as a bus cleaner or construction worker. Political protest is his full-time occupation, one that does not seem to have much of a future post-1997. With a low international profile, he is much more vulnerable than some other dissidents. Few people believe that Beijing would risk the international censure sure to occur if they moved against Lee. But would anyone notice if Leung disappeared?

"I'm a left-wing activist. I don't think that the international media will like me very much," he says candidly.

Leung describes himself as a Revolutionary Marxist—a Trotskyite. He leads an organization called the April 5 Movement (on that day in 1976 the first spontaneous demonstration against the communist regime took place in Tiananmen Square). The movement advocates direct elections to China's National People's Congress, workers' councils in factories and "political rights for all Chinese". It is one of the paradoxes of the transition that a person most at risk from the transfer to "Red" China should be another communist. No one believes for a moment that any prominent capitalists, such as billionaire Li Ka-shing, would be persecuted. Li and many other of his fellow tycoons already have an important say in the transition and are frequently touted for high-profile positions in the new Special Administrative Region.

Of course, it is by no means certain that Leung or any other person who demonstrates against China will be arrested after July, 1997. After all, the Basic Law, which Beijing promises to uphold, guarantees freedom of expression and assembly. A major test will be what happens to organizations like the April 5 Movement and especially the Alliance. The latter was formed in May, 1989, one month before the bloody crack down, to boost the flagging student protests with money and donations from Hong Kong. After the massacre, sympathizers in the territory helped hundreds of people to reach safety abroad. It is still very much a part of the Hong Kong scene, and every year on June 4, it organizes a memorial service honoring those who died.

This year's observance drew a large crowd of people for a candlelight vigil in Victoria Park, considerably more than have attended in recent years. Many of those holding candles must have felt that it might be the last public memorial. To be sure, on June 4, 1997, Hong Kong will still be under British administration, but there is a widespread belief that many of the venues will be closed for "renovation" in anticipation of the handover celebrations a few weeks later. This year Szeto Wah lit a flame and delivered a defiant eulogy: "This is for those who died seven years ago. The troops that butchered you will soon be on your soil. The tanks that crushed you will parade in the streets of Hong Kong, but we have no fear. We're determined that China will have democracy. And we will fight until the end."

Beijing's leaders have no reason to love the Alliance or its leaders, but they may be cautious about moving against them since they have considerable popular support in the territory. Beijing has never specifically labeled its activities as seditious (the local pro-Beijing press is not so circumspect), even though it officially condemns the pro-democracy advocates on the mainland as "counter-revolutionary". Last April when the Beijing-appointed Preparatory Committee extended an invitation to the Professional Teachers Association, headed by Szeto Wah, to address the committee on how the post-1997 chief executive should be chosen, it was seen as something of a peace offering. Unfortunately, the association loudly protested the decision to disband Legco and was quickly disinvited.

Article 23 of the Basic Law allows the new government to enact laws prohibiting acts of "treason and sedition against the Central People's Government". Whether these laws will address only violent actions, such as terrorism, or whether they might be aimed at mere advocacy is one of the uncertainties of the transition. It is also anticipated that the new government will restore some not-so-old colonial decrees that were sparingly used by the British to limit political activity in the colony.

"The Public Order ordinance used to require us to get police permits for assemblies of more than three persons. I don't think they need to make very big changes to it," said Leung. "They can use old weapons to control people."

"What do you plan to do to protect your selves after the hand-over?" I asked him.

"The majority of the committee hasn't decided exactly what we would do if we are arrested. They mainly say that we would fight in the courts. After that, it's not clear," said Leung, who didn't sound like he had much confidence in getting protection from the courts if Beijing truly were to repress his movement.

Of course, nearly a million of his fellow Hong Kong residents, anticipating such an eventuality, have taken the precaution of obtaining foreign passports or right to live abroad, but not Leung.

"I just have a British National Overseas document"—which allows him to travel but does not carry the right to live in Britain or anywhere else should things get too hot for him in Hong Kong. Even so, Leung says he will continue to agitate for democracy in China even after the handover.

"We won't disappear."

\*    \*    \*    \*

"The churches in Hong Kong have never experienced so many heavy issues," sighed Tso Man-king, the head of the Hong Kong Christian Council, which represents about half of the territory's mainline Protestant churches. Tso had spent several weeks this spring with his colleagues wrestling over whether to accept an invitation to send representatives to serve on the Selection Committee, the electoral college that will choose Hong Kong's first Chinese chief executive later this year. Some Christian leaders have serious reservations about doing anything to cooperate with the officially atheistic Chinese authorities. The churches also include many who have been active in the pro-democracy movement in Hong Kong, and they, naturally enough, harbor deep reservations about taking part in any exercise that seems to help Beijing in its goal to dismantle the elected legislature. As they see things, by joining the Selection Committee, Christians are not just being good citizens but are, in effect, being coopted politically by the authorities.

After a considerable amount of soul-searching, the Christian Council voted 32-5 on "principled" cooperation in helping form Hong Kong's new administration by forming a nominations committee. Tso told me that he hoped to finesse the provisional legislature issue by having the church representatives abstain from voting when the time comes to pick the 60 members who will serve on that body. The Roman Catholic hierarchy also agreed to serve, as did the Anglicans whose bishop, Peter Kwong, is a member of the Preparatory Committee and also served on the committee that drafted the Basic Law. "Being a good Christian also means being a good citizen," wrote Cardinal John Wu in a document called "Pastoral Guidelines for the 1997 Transition".

Christians make up only about 10 percent of Hong Kong's population, about equally divided between Protestants and Roman Catholics, but they provide social services out of proportion to their numbers. Protestant organizations, for example, operate three post-secondary colleges, 121 secondary and 146 primary schools plus seven hospitals and 61 social service organizations. The Catholic Church operates 397 schools, including some of the territory's most prestigious secondary institutions. Since the opening of the first orphanage in Hong Kong—to care for the offspring of European merchants and sailors—the churches have been deeply involved in providing social welfare services. Of the top ten non-governmental agencies receiving tax support, about half are Christian institutions; the schools get about 95 percent of their funding from the government. So one could say that churches are pretty solidly enmeshed with the secular authorities. Maybe too much.

What Hong Kong needs now are fewer people willing to cooperate with the emerging new order and more people "who can monitor and dare to criticize the increasingly powerful civil authorities controlled by a small group of people," declared Reverend Kwok Nai-wong. He once served as the general secretary of the Hong Kong Christian Council but left to form the Christian

Institute, which takes up the causes of the poor and disadvantaged. "The Selection Committee contravenes every principle of democracy which any church throughout the world must champion," he declared in the Institute's newsletter. "By entangling itself on the Selection Committee, the church in Hong Kong may well be abdicating its responsibility in safeguarding the basic rights of the masses in Hong Kong. China's totalitarian government is coming to Hong Kong. Undoubtedly those who toe its line will be handsomely rewarded, but for sure it will be done at the expense of the masses."

Beijing began courting religious leaders in Hong Kong in September 1995, when, for the first time, many clergymen found little red envelopes in their mail with invitations to attend the annual October 1 National Day function that celebrates the founding of the People's Republic. Clergy had never before been invited to the diplomatic function, and there was considerable buzz over who got the invites and who would attend. This spring several local Protestant leaders took it upon themselves to propose that the churches organize a special thanksgiving on October 1, giving Tso Man-king a few more headaches. This day has never been widely observed in Hong Kong beyond the handful of left-wing schools and branches of the Bank of China, certainly not in churches. Tso gave cautious support to the idea, when I asked him about it. "Of course, we don't want to celebrate if it means shouting 'Long Live Mao Zedong', but if it means merely elevating our national identity, our pride in being Chinese, then I don't mind."

I rang up one of the organizers, Dr. Lo Lung-kwong, head of the Theological Division of Chung Chi College in the Chinese University, and asked him why, in God's name, any Christian leaders would want to celebrate China's National Day?

"Traditionally, we in Hong Kong have had a colonial mentality," he explained pleasantly. For many years Christianity was viewed as a "foreign creed" and European missionaries part of the apparatus of imperialism. "We want to become *Chinese,* not just some ethnic group," he continued.

"There is a saying in China that 'you add one Christian and you subtract one patriot'. The October 1 celebration is viewed as showing that Hong Kong's people can be Christians and patriotic too. (In fact, in the absence of missionaries and with an increasing base in Chinese culture, the Christian church in China is no longer viewed by many as a foreign implant. Which may be one reason it has grown dramatically in the past decade, in spite of periodic clashes with the authorities.)

"China did not start on October 1, 1949. It's 5,000 years old. That day only marks the communist victory over the Nationalists in the civil war. It is purely a political holiday," said the Reverend Chu Yiu-ming, the liberal pastor of the large Chai Wan Baptist Church when I put the same question to him. Many of his parishioners are refugees from the communists and actually prefer to honor the Double Ten (October 10, birthday of the Chinese republic in 1911, and effectively Taiwan's national day).

"We must respect all of those individuals. The church should never try to control those views."

Isn't this all some kind of devious plot to divide and weaken the churches in the run-up to 1997? Tso doubted any deliberate intention on the part of Xinhua. After all, he pointed out, the provision that the Selection Committee have 100 members chosen from the "labor, social services and religious sectors" of the community has been a part of the Basic Law since it was promulgated in 1990. Nothing new or especially sinister about inviting church members to serve on it. Indeed, the Chinese were probably relieved that the Christian establishment agreed to cooperate. Otherwise, they might have had to make the appointments themselves and that surely would have caused a row. Nevertheless, Tso agreed that the issue has had the effect of dividing those who might be considered "friendly" to China from those that are "unfriendly".

Then in June an eleven-person delegation headed by Ye Xiaowen, the director of China's government Religious Affairs Bureau (RAB) arrived in the colony to spend a week meeting with local church leaders. Tso hosted a luncheon for the delegation on June 26, which was attended by about 100 Protestant church leaders and included members of the Baptist Church and Missionary Alliance, who are not members of the Council. The meeting was cordial; all niceties were observed. Tso gave Ye a wooden carving of a cross set in a bed of lilies, which he explained symbolized fertility and life. The director gave Tso an engraved silver tray.

For the most part, the director merely repeated in several different ways the regulations embodied in the Basic Law, which hold out the principle of mutual non-interference in each others' religious affairs. He said that the Hong Kong churches could maintain their international ties and contacts without having to worry about the mainland law that restricts such contacts. "The RAB will not send any religious organizations from China to work for Hong Kong nor apply any religious policy or rules and regulations that are in effect in China. It is not our expectation that the religious sectors adopt the socialist system. All we want is your respect and your patriotic devotion to your country," he said.

One of the church leaders asked him what would be needed for a foreigner or somebody from Hong Kong to go to preach in China.

He replied: "Same as now. You have to have an invitation from a recognized church or other religious institution, and the invitation must be approved by the local RAB branch." Again, he stressed, "We won't interfere with you, and you must not use your Hong Kong standards to impose [your values] on religious groups in China."

That sounds good. The problem is that many Christians consider it their moral duty to "interfere" in China's affairs. Conservative evangelicals, mainly from the US, deliberately violate China's laws by sending in clandestine missionaries or smuggling in Bibles, never mind that the Chinese churches have printed millions in the past decade. They boast about it in videos aimed at their home churches. Some groups especially active in nurturing the underground (nonregistered and thus technically illegal) churches in mainland China have decided that it is prudent to move their operations out of the colony. Cooperative Services International, an offshoot of the Southern Baptists, has moved to Singapore. Another group, China Ministries International which aids "house" churches and itinerant preachers, has moved to Taiwan. "I don't want our research and publishing work to be subjected to pressure," said founder Jonathan Chao.

Liberal clergymen also have some reasons to be concerned. For example, Reverend Chu is active in the Christian Industrial Council, one of Hong Kong's oldest labor groups. The latest issue of its newsletter *Change* criticizes child labor practices in China and advocates the formation of independent unions, anathema to the communists. Further, Chu is, like Leung a leader of the Alliance in Support of Patriotic Democratic Movements in China, which organizes observances commemorating the June 4 uprising.

"The 'suddenly-I-love-China' people tell us that China is China and Hong Kong is Hong Kong. If that is true, why is China always interfering in Hong Kong politics?" he asks. "Hong Kong's people have to believe in the 'one country, two systems' concept, but from the point of view of the church, things are not so clear. Because the church's mission is not like politics. We need to preach the Gospel to the whole world."

# July 1996 -365 DAYS

*"After 1997 we can tell China to take a hike."*

ONE YEAR TO GO. In Beijing, a handful of people watched and cheered as the count-down clock in Tiananmen Square changed from 366 to 365 days. "Today, under the leadership of the Chinese Communist Party, the people of China have stood up and will wash away a century of national shame," intoned the *People's Daily.* It did warn cadres, however, "not to interfere in the internal workings of the SAR government." Beijing songwriter Ren Zheping came up with a commemorative tune: *We will be reunited under the full moon.* In Hong Kong, the Democratic Party and the Democratic Alliance for the Betterment of Hong Kong marked the occasion with separate demonstrations in Central. The DAB entered Chater Gardens, where Tsang Yok-sing denounced everyone who "prophesied the end of Hong Kong". Then the Democrats held their all-night candlelight vigil. Following that, about 300 of them marched to the headquarters of Xinhua in Happy Valley to protest the plan to disband the legislature one year from today.

On the radio Chris Patten proclaimed that, "Britain has kept its word on democratic development in Hong Kong. It remains to be seen whether China will," which drew a retort from Xinhua deputy director Zhang Junsheng that it would be better for Patten to cooperate than to issue challenges. After 1997, the governor continued, people will still be free to demonstrate and write letters to newspapers "in the same way you do today." He encouraged them to do so. In a rare interview, Xinhua Director Zhou Nan took a similarly optimistic view.

BUSINESS AS USUAL, headlined the *South China Morning Post.*

Opposition groups, such as the Democratic Party will be tolerated, "so long as they obey the Basic Law". "Nothing changes on July 1,

1996, but the calendar means that Hong Kong's mind is now powerfully concentrated on what will happen in twelve months' time," wrote the *Post* in an editorial.

The local media are grumbling about how all of those big Chinese officials, such as Lu Ping and Zhou Nan, are giving one-year-to-go interviews to the international press and ignoring the locals. Of course, Lu Ping's interview with the international Cable News Network, CNN, didn't go as smoothly as he may have wanted. Lu had clearly wanted to say some reassuring things about how Hong Kong's traditional freedoms would be respected after the change of sovereignty. "They can criticize the [Chinese] government. They can object to our policies. They can say anything they like," he said. That sounded promising. But a questioner inevitably asked whether this freedom extended to writing articles or editorials advocating independence for Taiwan. "Absolutely not," Lu replied shaking his head for emphasis. On July 1, however, much of the Hong Kong media had its attention set on a somewhat more parochial story. Many front pages contained paid advertisements from local retailing tycoon Dickson Poon denying that he had terminal cancer and was in desperate search of a faith healer. *Sudden Weekly,* one of several publications owned by the new media magnate, Jimmy Lai, had evidently published a story to that effect, and then, reacting to Poon's fervent denials, and presumably threats of action for libel, finally admitted that the story had been a fabricated by an 18-year-old cub reporter.

Eight Democratic Party legislators and their supporters flew to Beijing on July 1 to deliver petitions protesting the disbanding of the legislature. They didn't even get off the plane: they were bundled into the first class compartment, questioned, had their home-visit permits canceled and then were denied entry into China for "national security" reasons. Interestingly, the airline, Dragonair, had allowed them to get on the aircraft at Hong Kong, evidently not influenced by the recent acquisition of a 35 percent stake by a Chinese state-owned airline. In 1993, Chinese dissident Han Dongfang had tried to return home this way, and all it took was a fax from Beijing saying that his passport had been canceled to prevent him from even boarding the aircraft in Hong Kong. Aside from the theater on the tarmac, the big news from this strange encounter was the three-page list that the Chinese authorities brandished. They called it a "flight manifest", though the petitioners promptly labeled it a "black list". The Chinese were happy to let the protesters take a peek at the list, which supposedly contained the names of such well-known liberals as Szeto Wah and Martin Lee and others who were not on the trip. It seemed to suggest that any active involvement in the Democratic Party would make it impossible for Hong Kong people to visit China.

At a luncheon at the Foreign Correspondents' Club, James Tien and Henry Tang, who had joined the chorus of businessmen's criticism of Patten for his *Newsweek* comments, were the speakers. Said Tang: "I expect there to be problems [concerning the handover]. Even with a merger like Chase Manhattan and Chemical Bank, there are problems." Many businessmen, he continued, have a healthy skepticism about 1997 but they "put their faith in the Basic Law." He went on to say that previously all issues that straddled 1997, like the airport, Container Terminal 9 and the Western Corridor Railway, had required complex international negotiations.

"After 1997 they become purely Hong Kong issues. We can tell them [China] to take a hike." We'll see.

\*     \*     \*     \*

How is confidence in the future holding up, one year before the handover date? Not bad, one would guess from reading the traditional indices. The main bellwethers, stock and property markets, are surging as well. The most expensive piece of land ever auctioned in Hong Kong was sold in March. No evidence of mass emigration. Indeed, what many had feared might turn into a mad scramble to get out of Hong Kong as the handover date approaches has turned into a stampede to get back in. The reason is that many Hong Kong

Chinese, who had obtained foreign citizenship as a hedge against
Communist Party repression, are returning home because they
think that they must be physically present in the territory before
July 1, 1997, if they want to live here without having to obtain a
residency visa and a work permit like any other foreigner. The
Canadians are already getting worried that the airlines in the weeks
leading to the handover will be fully booked, since Canada has
long been a favored destination for Hong Kong people wanting to
emigrate. It's been said that flights are already fully booked by
people desperate to get back *in* to Hong Kong—before it is too
late.

And it is not just Hong Kong émigrés. All kinds of people are
flocking to Hong Kong in this, its last year under British rule. The
population of expatriates here hit a low point in the years immediately following the signing of the Joint Declaration in 1984 and
the Tiananmen massacre in 1989, but it began to increase rapidly
in 1991. Perhaps not coincidentally, that was the year that Deng
Xiaoping's famous tour of Shenzhen and Guangdong province
rekindled China's market reforms, igniting the economy. Now the
expatriate population is probably double what it was in 1989. One
of the strangest phenomena is the rise in the resident British
population. In the year when one might expect that Britons would
be packing their bags and preparing to leave by next July, their
numbers are actually surging. They had bottomed out in 1987 at
about 18,000, lower even than Americans. Today, their numbers
are estimated to exceed 35,000—up nearly a quarter in the first five
months of 1996 alone. But the reason isn't all that mysterious.

Take Martin Amor, for example. A few weeks ago he was
working in a factory in South Wales. But the wages were very poor,
he says, so he decided to do what tens of thousands of his
countrymen have done for more than a hundred years—seek his
fortune in Hong Kong. He got a much better paying job working
as a mechanical supervisor at the mammoth airport construction
project. Now he literally lives on the "Gold Coast", a fancy new
seaside development that is popular with expatriates. Or take Peter

May, an engineer from Dover, who has been working for the past three years as an engineer, also at the airport construction site. "There's work here, and if you consider the options, it's a pretty good place to be." The Channel Tunnel, where he worked before coming to Hong Kong, was really the last major infrastructure project in Britain. And one more reason, "you hear it all of the time. People say, 'I want to see Hong Kong as it was, before it all changes forever.'"

Many of the new British migrants in Hong Kong, are, not to put too fine a point on it, from the working classes, and they are taking on what used to be dismissed as "coolie work", driving bulldozers, crushing rocks, tending bars, selling sandwiches in office buildings. In the earlier days of the colony, of course, Hong Kong did provide an outlet for the lower-class unemployed, those anyway who could afford to get here, and often a quick leg up into the middle classes. British people staffed the middle as well as upper levels of the civil service, becoming sanitary department inspectors or police superintendents, or the like. Beginning in the 1980s, however, the government began seriously to purge the civil service of foreigners in a "localization" program designed to replace jobs that were once filled by British expats with local Chinese.

In the early days, too, no self-respecting Brit or other European would want to be seen working with his hands. The goal was to be an overseer or some kind of technician. But these days no stigma is attached to "coolie work", and these new migrants seem happy enough to take jobs that would have been socially unacceptable, even 20 years ago. Because of the rapid rise in wealth throughout Asia, and in Hong Kong in particular, even fairly menial jobs now pay as much or more than equivalent jobs in Britain. Indeed, per capita income is now higher in Hong Kong than it is "back home".

Remarkably few complaints are heard from the Chinese population about the influx. Some union leaders and their representatives in Legco have grumbled about Brits taking away jobs that could go to the locals. "These people are swarming into Hong Kong like bees," observed the left-wing newspaper *Wen Wei Po,* the other day.

Other complaints concern loutish behavior on ferry boats to Lantau Island, where many British and other foreign construction workers live relatively cheaply, three or four to a villa. But there doesn't seem to be a great deal of open resentment. Jobs are generally plentiful these days, and, in any case, the window will soon slam shut. After the handover, British people will be obliged to obtain residency visas and work permits like any other foreigner, including the many who are already here on automatic one-year residency permits. Employers will have to prove that they cannot find a local to do the job, which ought to be nearly impossible for non-skilled work and pretty difficult for the semi-skilled.

*      *      *      *

Since 1993, Michael DeGolyer and his team at the Hong Kong Transition Project at the Baptist University have been taking the pulse of Hong Kong people's hopes and fears every six months. His latest polling was made this July and shows, he says, that despite the superficial indicators many people still harbor worries, fears and anxieties that could prove troublesome for the incoming administration. "Over the years, we've found that a fairly consistent one quarter of the population desires that Hong Kong rejoin China. The rest have various doubts." This is a pretty thin reed for building a new and stable society, he says. The figure has crept up slowly, but it should at least be in the 40 to 50 percent range. Still, he says, there are some numbers in his polling from which China could take heart. The expectation of a Chinese-stimulated economic boom after the handover is growing (and with it the fear of a bust to follow.) The feeling that the levels of service will decline and that the new government will perform more poorly than the present British administration is slowly receding—except in one crucial area, corruption. "It tops the list."

The main test of confidence will come if, despite the present trends, large numbers of people decide to leave. An extraordinary number have over the years have acquired means of getting out in a hurry, even though the outflow of Hong Kong people to safe-haven countries such as Canada has subsided in recent years. Ever since DeGolyer's first survey was conducted in February 1993, a consistent six percent of the respondents have indicated that they possess a foreign passport. That seems small, but the number of people who could get out of Hong Kong increases dramatically if one includes relatives living abroad who can provide sponsorships. Nearly half of Hong Kong's population have some family members living abroad, not including China or Taiwan, DeGolyer estimates. So probably as many as 40 or 50 percent probably could arrange to leave if they felt things were not going right, he said.

What could cause people to leave? DeGolyer said the most critical issue is a feeling of loss of personal freedom. "People tend to say that so long as the economy is doing fine, so long as people are making money, everything will be okay. It's not true. The SAR and the Chinese governments can't afford to assume that they have a wide base of support or that most people would stay in Hong Kong under any circumstances." The bottom line, he says, is cautious optimism about the future. When asked: Do you think there will truly be Hong Kong people ruling Hong Kong after 1997, about 51 percent respond only with "a slight chance".

"It's utterly dependent on what China does," he concluded. "The more they live up to the promises made in the Joint Declaration and the Basic Law, the more likely there will be a successful transition. The more the PRC is perceived to be the power behind the throne, the more likely that people will exercise their options and leave."

\*   \*   \*   \*

Lau Ah-kouk made a flying leap from the roof of a stone hut into a sea of riot policemen and journalists, injuring himself and one of the cops. It didn't do him any good; he was still evicted. Lau was one of the last holdouts at Rennie's Mill, a village on Junk Bay on Kowloon Peninsula that was the famous home for 40 years to about

7,000 ex-soldiers of Chiang Kai-shek's defeated Nationalist army and their families. After their final evictions on July 30, the village was padlocked, and the population was redistributed to efficient, if nondescript public housing blocks. The government steadfastly denies that Rennie's Mill had to go because the incoming administration won't tolerate the presence of such a partisan enclave. It all has to do with the need for more housing, it claims. But most people are sure that the government simply could not permit the continued existence of this "little Taiwan".

On one level, it is a familiar Hong Kong story. The government has cleared numerous squatters villages in this manner over the years. Most of the villagers, like those in the Kowloon Walled City redevelopment last year, took their government compensation and moved on to more modern accommodations. Only about 500 or so Rennie's Mill diehards resisted the government inducements—and punishments, such as closing the schools, turning off the water—and held out until their last appeal before the High Court over proper compensation was exhausted last month and the police moved in. But Rennie's Mill is very different from the dozens of other squatter settlements, created from the spillover of refugees that poured into Hong Kong following the formation of the People's Republic of China in 1949.

The community traces its history to 1949 when remnants of Chiang's defeated army sought refuge in the colony. They were first settled in Kennedy Town on the western side of Hong Kong Island, but after fighting with some communist sympathizers, it was decided to move them to a remote corner of the Kowloon peninsula, where, presumably, they could live without causing any further trouble. So on June 26, 1950 a flotilla of government ferries brought the refugees to Rennie's Mill—so called because it was on the site of an old flour mill, once owned by a Canadian, Alfred Rennie, who had committed suicide when his business went bankrupt. The mill was torn down in 1923. The Kuomintang followers were herded into a crowded refugee camp without water, electricity, roads or regular ferry service. They managed over the years to create a tightly-knit community; schools were established, complete with pictures of Chiang and Sun Yat-sen; shacks were converted over time into stone cottages and restaurants. Many of the villager got by on small remittances from Taipei, although the Nationalists were never very generous. Taipei stopped sending pensions—which at approximately us$25 a month weren't much anyway—last June.

To get there I took a subway to Choi Hung station in Kowloon and then boarded mini bus No. 290, the last day of service, as it turned out. It dropped me off at the entrance to the village, where one lonely Nationalist flag flew defiantly behind a government sign announcing that the property was condemned and that anyone who trespassed did so at his own risk. I didn't venture deeply into the maze of broken glass and boarded up windows. Off to the left and down a rather steep hill, I could see the flat, rectangular dirt pallet of a land reclamation project, and behind it the construction cranes working on a new public housing block. Soon the name Rennie's Mill will be only a memory. The stone cottages will be torn down and the area subsumed into the massive Tseung Kwan O New Town, which is being built nearby and will eventually be home for half-a-million people. They will have all the attributes of modern Hong Kong: a subway stop, a Home Ownership Scheme and a branch of a Japanese department store.

# September 1996 -303 DAYS

*"I only hear the term 'pro-Beijing' in Hong Kong. We prefer to be called 'patriotic'."*

"WE SINCERELY HOPE that people from all walks of life in Hong Kong will participate in the Selection Committee and be fully dedicated to the future of Hong Kong by exercising their rights and making contributions to the smooth transition." So read the advertisements in the newspapers and on television as nominations opened for appointment to the 400-member electoral college that will choose Hong Kong's first Chinese chief executive later this year. Taking them up on the offer, I went down to the Preparatory Committee Secretariat's main office at the corner of Pedder Street and Queen's Road, (same building as Li Ka-shing's Cheung Kong property concern) to pick up an application form. Although supposedly 4,000 forms were taken during the first weekend, the office was not doing a booming business when I arrived. A couple of bored newspaper reporters camped out on the leather sofa sprang to life when they saw a foreigner applying for the committee. Then they began asking me questions and taking my picture. "I'm just here out of curiosity." From what I could see from the application form, the requirements for becoming an elector were not very demanding ... "Members of the Selection Committee must satisfy the following qualifications and conditions: uphold the principle of 'one country, two systems' and the Basic Law and be willing to perform the functions and duties of the Selection Committee, namely to recommend a candidate for the office of the first chief executive and to elect members of the Provisional Legislative Council."

The weekend before nominations opened brought considerable soul-searching over whether organizations could, in good conscience, nominate people to serve because one of the duties is to elect the hotly controversial provisional legislature. The Hong Kong Journalists Association to which I belong decided it would not nominate any members as part of the labor contingent. But if I wanted to apply, it would verify that I was a member. The Democratic Party, as expected, pledged to boycott the committee, despite Foreign Minister Qian Qichen's explicit invitation to take part, issued a few days before nominations opened. Its rival, the DAB, had no qualms about participating, although it seemed to me that Tsang Yok-sing tied himself up in knots last night on television trying to justify his party's decision. As best I could figure, his reasoning went like this: the DAB supports the need for the provisional legislature because Britain violated the Basic Law in unilaterally drawing up new election rules. But the party also supports the concept of an elected legislature. Ergo, the provisional legislature is an elected legislature and so the DAB can nominate members.

Some suggest that the dilemma could be finessed by simply not voting when the provisional legislature vote comes up. That was the preferred course of the Christians who had specifically conditioned their decision to join the Selection Committee on abstaining when the time came to pick the provisional legislators. Some had suggested that the Democrats might follow this course, too. Yet, the Declaration on the application form states quite unequivocally: "I am willing to perform the two duties of the Selection Committee." How could anyone sign that statement in good conscience while planning to avoid acting on one of the jobs? Party Vice Chairman Yeung Sum said, "We will not consider joining the committee and then abstaining on the issue of the provisional legislature because then the Democrats would be involving themselves in the very process of forming an illegal body." Despite these reservations, quite a large number of people have shown an interest in this election. Some 20,000 took out forms (including me) and about 5,800 returned them (not including me). The Chinese have reason to be pleased. The more people that participate in this peculiar election, the more it will be perceived as fair and open. That will in turn confer an important sense of legitimacy on whoever is finally selected to be Hong Kong's first Chinese governor.

If the chief were selected by a direct vote of all Hong Kong citizens, Anson Chan would be the winner today. Opinion polls consistently show that the career civil servant—whom Patten made his deputy and head of the civil service—would win overwhelmingly against either the purported front-runner, Tung Chee-hwa, or dark horse candidate T.S. Lo, or anyone else, including even Martin Lee. The *Post* reported in August that 51 percent of Hong Kong's people favored her. Tung was barely into single digits after more than six months of intense speculation about his candidacy. A few months ago Chan looked like a dead duck. She supposedly was done in by her loyal support of Patten on his opposition to the provisional legislature. An undercurrent of unease about Tung because of his business connections and closeness to billionaire Li may has given her candidacy some new life. But Preparatory Committee members have made things extremely difficult by suggesting that if she really wants the job, she should resign her high position. As a civil servant, she should not be seen as taking part in politics, it is suggested. It would be a hard choice, because she could lose everything if she is not chosen. And she remains a long-shot at best. She is still considered too close to the outgoing British administration and generally too "Western" in outlook. On the other hand, keeping her on as chief secretary after 1997 is increasingly seen as fundamental to retaining confidence.

So for the moment, Tung remains very much the favorite, as he has been all year. People now believe that the grooming process began as far back as 1992, after Tung was appointed to the Executive Council (Exco), the governor's inner cabinet of advisers. Patten was beginning a confrontation with China over political reforms and it had seemed advisable to appoint an Exco member perceived to be on friendly terms with Beijing. By that time Tung was already a member of the Chinese People's Political Consultative Conference, the national-level advisory body. Indeed, he was the first openly "pro-Beijing" figure ever appointed to Exco. Tung's excellent

Beijing connections stemmed, of course, from the timely infusion of US$120 million into his business in the mid-1980s negotiated by "old China Friend" Henry Fok, saving his shipping empire, Orient Overseas, from bankruptcy. Therein lies a tale.

Tung inherited the family business in 1983 shortly before a disastrous freight price war erupted. His father, C.Y. Tung, had a penchant for buying expensive supertankers and container ships, not to mention such extravagances as the *Queen Elizabeth* luxury liner that he converted into a "floating university". That saddled the company with debts of more than US$2.5 billion. At first Tung Chee-hwa approached the Taiwan government for help, hoping to make good use of ties between his late father and the island's Nationalist government. But he was turned down because Taipei had earlier let a local shipping company go bankrupt, and injecting cash into Tung's line would have invited criticism for favoritism. It was then that Fok offered to help him find a lifeline in Beijing. Orient Overseas received two infusions of cash: one was a US$100 million standby loan through the Hongkong and Shanghai Banking Corporation (of which Tung is a director) to help repay individual creditors, half of it provided by the Bank of China. The second was a US$120 million personal investment by Fok.

The extent to which this puts Tung in Beijing's debt, is, of course, a question that continues to hang over his candidacy. It should be noted that the loans and investments were a fraction of the shipping line's total indebtedness, though it was key to restructuring the others. It may be that Beijing authorities were looking ahead ten years to the man they'd like to groom for chief. It is equally plausible, however, that they then saw it more as a way of establishing good connections to help rebuilt their own shipping line at a time when China was rapidly increasing its exports. The man who was probably most influential in helping arrange the bailout was the then Premier Zhao Ziyang, who was overthrown seven years ago in the wake of Tiananmen and has not been in a position of influence for some time.

By the early 1990s, Tung's business enterprises had recovered to the point where he could contemplate a public career. David Chu, a businessman who also has strong links to China, thinks that Tung began to entertain serious ambitions about becoming chief about two years ago. As Chu put it to me during one of our breakfast meetings, "He must have thought to himself, 'My business is okay, and I'm the highest ranking Hong Kong government official who happens to have the best relations with China.'" Another longtime observer described Tung to me as a kind of balancer. "He knew how to balance British and Chinese interests." Of course, the perception of being acceptable both to the British—and presumably to Hong Kong—and to China, is still perhaps Tung's strongest asset.

Of course, Tung has another important advantage, the apparent backing of President Jiang Zemin. They presumably met in early 1989, when the shipping magnate brought his floating university to Shanghai. Jiang was then the local Communist Party chieftain, shortly before Deng Xiaoping brought him to Beijing and installed him as party general secretary. In January, this year, Tung went to Beijing for the inaugural meeting of the Preparatory Committee, on which he serves as one of four vice chairmen. President Jiang seemed to go out of his way to shake hands with him. Videos taken of the scene show Jiang scanning the crowd, obviously looking for a familiar face, then thrusting his hands out to greet Tung.

Throughout the year, Tung has maintained a very low profile. Not only has he not publicly declared his intention of seeking the post, he has not said *anything* in public, although his resignation from Exco on June 3 spoke louder than any formal declaration. It was seen as a way to put some distance between the Patten administration and him. Also rumors circulated that perhaps he did not really want the job. It is difficult to determine whether this apparent reticence stems from a self-effacing nature or whether, as seems more likely, it was tactical. Of course, it doesn't hurt to seem reluctant at this stage of the game. It may be a ploy to win some concessions from Beijing. Or, it may be that he does have some

serious personal reservations. What if the Democrats chain themselves to their Legco desks next July 1 and refuse to be budged—all
in the face of 5,000 journalists and cameramen from around the
world? Who needs that?

"Don't rule out the 'great survivor'," writes Danny Gittings in
his *Post* column. The great survivor is Lo Tak-shing, who makes
no secret that he thinks he would do a good job as Hong Kong's
first chief. His speech at the *Far Eastern Economic Review*'s
"Countdown to '97" conference this summer was seen as a kind
of campaign kickoff. Despite being a very pro-British member of
Exco, Lo has tried to position himself as the most "pro-Beijing"
candidate in the field. In 1992 he founded a weekly newsmagazine
called *Window*, and has been bankrolling it through all these
money-losing years mainly for the purpose of currying favor in
Beijing. Somewhere along the line too he managed to acquire
Chinese citizenship, which is not supposed to be available to Hong
Kong people. His main argument would likely be that he can
somehow "explain" the Hong Kong position to the Chinese.

The *Asia Times* quotes "mainland sources" as saying it is a
certainty that Lo—"the most unpopular figure in Hong Kong"—
will become the next chief because he is the only figure that Beijing
really trusts. Lo wrote an astonishingly harsh attack on Patten in
the overseas edition of the *People's Daily* using many terms and
phrases that are favorite themes with the Chinese Communist
Party propaganda bureau. In the article entitled, "A Highly Efficient Government—the Key to Hong Kong People Ruling Hong
Kong", he attacked the governor, claiming that he was behind a
conspiracy to bring "turmoil" to the territory. "These are just
typical policies by a colonial regime about to withdraw, or perhaps
this is a part of the Western powers' strategy to slow down China's
development. Under Patten, civil service confidence was shaken,
Hong Kong's prudent financial management system was abandoned and pressure was put on the dollar." He even accused Patten
of eating into the territory's billions in reserves. "All this leaves the
first SAR government a very difficult task of rebuilding." The

outburst brought a rare public rebuke from Anson Chan, who accused Lo himself of undermining confidence in the territory. Even China's official spokesmen seemed to distance themselves from the article. Both the Foreign Ministry and Xinhua pointed out that these were Lo's personal views. Chinese foreign ministry spokesman Shen Guofang, told one local television station that the chief should be someone acceptable to all sides, including Britain. That was about as close as he came to saying that a successful candidate should be anyone but Lo.

So what to make of Lo? It would be easy to write him off as a spoiler. But political commentator Andy Ho thinks he may play an important role in the selection, even if he is not chosen himself. Over the years, he has forged close ties with powerful elements in the New Territories, where he helped the indigenous people get land entitlements. And it is notable that the New Territories Association of Societies picked up the largest number of forms— some 500—when Selection Committee nominations opened on August 14. Conceivably, he might be able to persuade 50 members to nominate him. He is also said to have the support of Lee Shau-kee, the colony's richest businessman, which is no small thing. But in the end it seems he can do nothing more than play the spoiler. He has some obvious disadvantages that make it almost impossible to conceive that he might be chosen: he's unpopular in Hong Kong, he's Eurasian, and he's a life-long (until recently) anglophile who seems to have acquired his "Chineseness" too quickly.

In early September the complexion of the race changed considerably when Chief Justice Sir Ti Liang Yang joined. Yang was out of the colony sailing in the Mediterranean on a cruise ship (not the greatest place to be when announcing one's candidacy) when a Preparatory Committee member and pro-Beijing magazine publisher, Xu Simin, announced that he would nominate him. Since then, "Sir T.L." has resigned from the judiciary and taken to calling himself just plain Yang Ti-liang. He had enjoyed a brief blip of speculation late last year at about the time that Anson Chan's star and that of other civil servants seemed on the rise. But then he seemed to scotch his chances when he tied himself up in verbal knots trying to explain away some negative comments he reportedly had made at a private dinner with the Xinhua deputy director, Zhang Junsheng. Discussing the then controversial plan to gut the Bill of Rights, Sir T.L. told Zhang that he thought the Bill of Rights hampered police in some ways. In itself this was not such a remarkable comment. Many prominent people make no excuses for opposing to the Bill of Rights. But Yang's rather clumsy efforts to explain himself called into question whether he has enough political judgment to be an effective chief executive.

Two schools of thought surround the Yang candidacy. One holds that the decision on who should be the new chief has already been decided in Tung's favor by the powers that be. Yang's candidacy is just window-dressing, designed to give the appearance of a "race". That is basically the line taken by many liberals in the colony, including independent legislator Emily Lau, who loudly maintains that the whole selection process is a farce. Another school holds that his entry is the clearest indication yet that the race is not at all cut-and-dried. With only 300 or so days left, Beijing has not yet come up with its final choice. Quite possibly it sees several candidates now announced or soon to declare as "acceptable". It will thus allow the Selection Committee process to take its course. None of the key Chinese authorities has told anyone definitively that they favor Tung. And a critical segment of opinion in the unions and the traditional left-wing community has always been uncomfortable with the idea of a businessman becoming the new chief. Beijing knows that the higher level of the tycoon community is a minefield of jealousies and rivalries.

"Some feel that Tung is too close to billionaire Li Ka-shing," says Andy Ho. "They worry that they might end up competing with Li but also with the future governor." A lot of people are unhappy with the way Li sold his satellite TV operation to a foreigner, Rupert Murdoch, and he is also tainted with the controversial Oriental Plaza development in Beijing." So Yang raises again the prospect of a "neutral" chief, chosen from the professional classes. Unlike Anson Chan, he has not had to defend Patten. And, as his unguarded comments on the Bill of Rights have shown, he is probably "sound" from Beijing's point of view, too.

*     *     *     *

Are the Chinese trying to make up with the Democrats? Foreign Minister Qian Qichen extended an olive branch on August 10 by inviting Democrats to put themselves forward for the Selection Committee. It seemed to be a signal that Beijing is willing to work with those with whom it disagrees. The Democrats politely declined. But significantly even this refusal did not provoke the usual outburst of criticism from the leftist press. Indeed, a sense of optimism is spreading through the pro-democracy camp despite its failure to budge the Chinese on certain issues dear to them, like the disbanding of the legislature. Less talk makes the rounds of their being forced to go into exile or chaining themselves to their Legco seats rather than surrender them to the provisional legislature next year.

If one considers Beijing's priorities to be, first, defusing "land mines" of the British and only later trying to win the hearts and minds of the Hong Kong people, this overture has logic. By now, Beijing must have decided that the soon-to-be-departing colonialists can do little more harm. So they can safely switch priorities back to mending relations with the Democrats, who, after all, have shown no inclination to leave. Other straws float in the wind: the pro-Beijing publisher Xu Simin had lunch with Martin Lee recently, ostensibly to ask his advice on matters pertaining to the stationing of PLA troops in Hong Kong. Rumors also circulate that Lee and his principal deputy, Yeung Sum, might go to Beijing some time before the end of the year. Party vice chairman Anthony Cheung, it is said, has already been there to lay the groundwork. Certainly, it would be one of the most celebrated trips since Richard Nixon visited Beijing in 1972.

The burst of patriotism over continued Japanese occupation of the Diaoyu Islands in the East China Sea, claimed by China, was also a heaven-sent opportunity for the Democrats to show their love for the motherland. Pro-democracy legislator Szeto Wah was photographed entering the Xinhua headquarters in Happy Valley to present a petition calling on Beijing to take stronger action to oust the Japanese from the uninhabited islets. It was the first time he had ever been inside China's Hong Kong inner sanctum. Then Tsang Kin-shing, another Democratic Party legislator and perpetual demonstrator, met with Tung to ask the shipping magnate's help in obtaining a ship to sail protesters to the islands. But it was also a useful occasion for the purported front-runner to meet with some members of the Democratic Party opposition.

Meanwhile, the liberal camp, never totally united, is showing more division. In August, Emily Lau announced she was forming her own political group—not a party, she insisted—named the Frontier. She issued a fiery manifesto: "At this critical juncture in the colony's history, Hong Kong people must decide whether they want to defend the high degree of [promised] autonomy or allow the SAR to be run by surrogates of the Chinese government. Our vision of Hong Kong in the 21st century is that it should be a vibrant and dynamic cosmopolitan city with respect for democracy, human rights and the rule of law. Despite the current difficulties, we will not abandon our long-held ideals and principles. Our main principle is that Hong Kong people should have the right to elect their own government." By this she means direct election of the chief executive, the legislature and Hong Kong's representatives to China's National People's Congress. Lau's liberal colleague, Christine Loh, on the other hand, seems to have adopted a different strategy. She abstained from the motion that condemned as unrepresentative the Preparatory Committee handling of the transition. She avoided the demonstrations that occurred during Lu Ping's April visit. Instead, Xinhua accepted her hand-delivered petition voicing opposition to the abolition of Legco. Then she even joined the Better Hong Kong Foundation, a pro-China business group.

With less than a year to go, the various forces in the liberal camp are obviously repositioning themselves and examining the best tactics to survive in a new system. The fear of arrest or exile may to be fading, but the liberals will be in the political wilderness for at least a year until the first post-1997 elections are held. They will be cut off from their constituencies, unable to make motions in the legislature or to intercede with the government to help their constituents. That makes it difficult to maintain a position from which to campaign effectively when elections are held, probably in 1998. Add to that, the Provisional Legislature will likely end the first-past-the-post voting system, making it harder for the Democrats to sweep the board as they have in the past.

\* \* \* \*

The sound of reggae music blares out of the sound truck as it crisscrosses Macau. I can just make out the words to "everything is gonna be all right," from Bob Marley's hit song. I'm in the Portuguese enclave on a rainy weekend in September to observe the election to the Legislative Assembly, the last one before the enclave (the first thing residents tell you is to never call Macau a colony) reverts to China on December 20, 1999, two-and-a-half years after Hong Kong. I want to see how the transition is proceeding. By reputation it's going a lot smoother here than in Hong Kong, with nothing comparable to the fight between Patten and China over democratic reforms. For this reason, the legislators being chosen this month will serve a special five-year term, which will take it to 2001. In Hong Kong parlance, the legislators will be riding the "through train" past 1999.

Macau actually has a longer tradition of voting than Hong Kong. Elections to the legislature were first introduced as far back as 1976—the first ones in Hong Kong weren't until 1991. Some say that the voting habit goes back even further, to the time when Europeans picked local councillors for the Leal Senado, the Loyal Senate, whose gleaming white building still dominates the central

plaza. But Macau has stayed with the original electoral arrangement, in which only eight of the 23 seats are elected directly, eight
are picked from functional constituencies and seven are still appointed by the Portuguese governor.

Perhaps because this is the last election under Portuguese rule,
it has attracted an unusual number of candidates. A dozen groups
have formed slates of candidates to contest the election. They go
by such vacuous names as the "Alliance for the Promotion of
Progress" (Macau's largest pro-China grassroots organization, with
two legislators) the "Association for the Promotion of Macau's
Success" (representing new immigrants from Fujian province in
China) to the "General Alliance for the Development of Macau"
(real estate and gambling). For the next two days our group, which
included about 25 Hong Kong journalists, four of us foreigners,
criss-crossed the peninsula meeting with every candidate. We
clambered off the bus and crowded into their campaign office.
There the four, five, six, or seven candidates sat at the front of the
table, while their leader presented their manifesto, usually in
Cantonese. If it was a businessman's group, the meeting might be
in a hotel room, refreshments and coffee served by uniformed
waiters. If a union or democracy group, it took place in their
cramped one-room campaign headquarters in a back-alley apartment building, and no refreshments.

Everyone seems to be ganging up against the entrenched pro-
Beijing camp, known in Macau as the "traditional forces". "I only
hear the term 'pro-Beijing' in Hong Kong," said legislator Tong
Chi-kin. "We prefer to be called 'patriotic'." He is a member of the
"Alliance for Development", which sounds a little better in
Chinese—the "One-Heart Promotion Association". But by whatever name they go by, the combination of leftist unions and
neighborhood associations has long dominated politics here. In
this election, Macau's business interests are making a concerted
effort to wrest seats from them. More than half of the slates
represent business groups, mostly real-estate interests or gambling,
the twin pillars of the local economy. The legislature already has

several seats reserved for "entrepreneurial" interests. "We feel that is too few," said Fong Chi-keong, a real estate salesman. Under Macau's proportional voting system, it is very difficult for any one slate to win more than one or at most two seats.

Another reason for the unusual business interest in this election is, of course, the impending handover. Unlike Hong Kong with its businessman-dominated Preparatory Committee, Macau's commercial sectors have fewer channels through which to influence the transition. The Assembly is, in a sense, the only game in town. Moreover, another fast-approaching date—2001—is almost as significant to Macau as 1999. That is the when the "franchise", as they call the gambling and casino monopoly, runs out. The candidates were adept at dodging questions on this delicate matter. As one said to me, "There're no votes in it. Too many people are dependent on the casinos. Me, too, I work for Uncle Ho."

Several of the slates have a more than passing interest in the matter. One purporting to represent the interests of the large number of recent immigrants from Fujian province is headed by a man who runs a tour operation bringing in gamblers from China, an increasingly large part of the business. Another was made up entirely of casino workers, who, to hear the bill of complaints from their press conference, don't think much of "Uncle" Stanley Ho's employment practices. The actual transition to Chinese rule figured only marginally in the campaign. Indeed, the economy is probably the main issue. Unemployment is officially 4.7 percent but some think it is higher. The property market has been vastly overbuilt in recent years resulting in a glut of empty apartments.

The legislative "through train" is one sign that the transition to Chinese sovereignty is progressing more smoothly than in Hong Kong. Many Macau residents can afford to be sanguine about the handover because Lisbon gave passports and the right of abode in Portugal (and by extension all of the European Community) to every person born in the territory. However, it only applies to those born here. The status of the large numbers of recent immigrants is unclear. Candidates of all persuasions agreed that "localization" of the civil service, still largely Portuguese, is moving far too slowly. By contrast, in Hong Kong virtually all of the top administrative posts have been held by ethnic Chinese for several years. "The situation may be like in Mozambique—suddenly the lower ranks move up," legislator Wang Chan-nam said. The Portuguese never pushed the local Chinese population to learn their language, and the Chinese never had much incentive to learn it either. So, translation of statutes, especially important court procedures, is moving slowly.

After the 1974 revolution in Portugal, Lisbon abandoned its colonial empire and tried to give Macau back to China; Beijing said the time was inappropriate. Ever since it has been officially described as "Chinese territory under Portuguese administration". There lies the fundamental difference in attitudes between the Portuguese and British to their former colonies. The Portuguese look on themselves as caretakers, generally willing to do the wishes of the future owners. The British, in their hearts, still think of themselves as owners, and they will bloody well do what they please up to midnight June 30, 1997.

"The Portuguese," he said, "do not see 1999 as the end of something but the beginning of a new relationship. After all, they agreed on the question of Chinese sovereignty long ago, while the British were still thinking of Hong Kong as a colony," said Edmund Ho, general manager of the Tai Fung Bank, vice president of the Assembly and oft-touted candidate for first Macau chief executive, when I asked him to explain the differing approaches of the Portuguese and British.

"Moreover, Portuguese business interests here are relatively insignificant compared with the British in Hong Kong. But Lisbon thinks that if the transition is handled smoothly, they'll have a special place in the China market."

So, how does he see the transition going compared with Hong Kong?

"There are still a lot of issues to be resolved. Not everything is 100 percent settled. But in Macau there is a consensus to try to work things out behind closed doors. The British say, 'if we disagree, we'll publicize it so that the Hong Kong people know we're fighting for them.' Macau is too small. It is not in a position to absorb the damage from confrontation."

# October 1996

*"Newspapers do fall prey to excitement."*

C HRIS PATTEN SAYS HE IS "GOBSMACKED", reported *Post* columnist Jonathan Braude, over negative reactions from legislators and the community to what was, in effect, his and Britain's farewell address to Hong Kong in Legco on October 4. He had hardly left the chamber before members were telling reporters how much they disliked it. Inchcape chief and Chamber of Commerce representative Paul Cheng pronounced it "condescending", while liberal solicitor Margaret Ng, also a Legco member, called it "patronizing". Emily Lau, predictably, blasted the speech because Patten didn't promise that the British government would save the current legislature from being disbanded and replaced by the provisional legislature. Never mind that the governor heaped scorn on the appointed body, claiming "it is unnecessary as well as provocative, and we will have nothing to do with it." For the first time in anybody's memory, the legislature failed to pass a resolution of thanks after the governor's address.

It is hard to understand exactly what the legislators and other opinion leaders found so condescending in the governor's last policy address. Certainly Patten was generous in praising Hong Kong and proclaiming his confidence in the future—Hong Kong is slated to become the "New York of Asia", he said—without claiming, at least not directly, that every good must have been Britain's doing. Not unless one reads that into such references as bestowing the "rule of law" as being completely self-serving. Naturally, he dwelt at some length about his own administration's accomplishments: "We cut pollution in rivers and streams in the New Territories by 70 percent through the livestock waste control scheme"—yes, and how the pig farmers squealed about it. He gave some rather vague assurances that Britain would continue to maintain its interest in Hong Kong's future, along the lines of John Major's "you'll never walk alone" speech during a visit earlier this year.

No doubt the businessmen in the legislature caught Patten's remark that "My anxiety is this: not that this community would be usurped by Peking, but that it would be given away bit by bit by some people in Hong Kong. We all know that over the past couple of years, we have seen decisions taken in the interest of the whole community lobbied against behind closed doors by those whose personal interests may have been personally affected." This may have reminded some of his earlier controversial interview with *Newsweek* magazine. How many times have businessmen gone to Beijing and assured leaders there that Hong Kong people have no special interest in democracy or in maintaining an independent press or any other freedoms, so long as they can continue to make money?

The governor also laid down sixteen "benchmarks" by which to judge whether Hong Kong's promised 50 years of autonomy and the preservation of personal freedoms, as promised in the Joint Declaration, will be carried out: "Is Hong Kong's civil service still professional and meritocratic? Are Hong Kong's courts continuing to operate without interference?" Of course, this whole attitude that "the world is watching" is extremely grating to Beijing, its supporters in Hong Kong, and possibly many Hong Kong people as well. They find it insulting that they must somehow conform to behavior set down by the departing colonizers. Never mind that many of these benchmarks—such as "are annual commemorations and vigils of recent years (by that, read the June 4 observances) still being allowed?"—are of great concern to many Chinese people here, not just to Western expatriates.

Three days earlier business tycoon Peter Woo gave what amounted to his own policy address, while announcing his candidacy for chief executive. It is interesting to compare these speeches and the reactions to them. Woo's address was received far more positively even though, if read side-by-side, they seem to say similar things. Woo acknowledged even more forthrightly than did Patten that people in Hong Kong are genuinely concerned about whether the concept of "one country, two systems" can become a reality and the extent to which China will refrain from intervening in Hong Kong's affairs. "They're worried as to whether or not the same rule of law will prevail, whether criminal elements here and across the border will collude and whether corruption and bribery will spread and whether law and order can be maintained. These concerns are real and have to be addressed."

He too talked about maintaining the civil service and upholding the principle of a level playing field in business affairs. His proposal to add some appointed members to district boards was perhaps his major departure from Patten's line and drew some immediate flak from the Democrats. But all in all, it was remarkably similar in tone. Yet Woo was praised, not criticized, for putting his political thoughts on record. Perhaps it is because he represents the Hong Kong to be born; Patten, representing the Hong Kong that was, would be criticized no matter what he said. Still, the governor's popularity seems to be holding up. In a recent poll, 67 percent expressed satisfaction with the way he is doing his job. But within the establishment, it may be that his welcome is wearing thin. "Perhaps the truth of the matter is that, as he enters his last nine months here, the governor is doomed by the calendar to lose consequence in the public eye," commented a *Post* editorial.

At least Beijing decided to be civil with the governor on the eve of his departure. After several months of negotiations it has been agreed that China's top official handling Hong Kong can shake hands with Patten at the ceremony marking the colony's return to China. "I have confirmed from Lu Ping that he is looking forward to shaking the hand of the governor at the ceremony," intoned Britain's Minister in Charge of Hong Kong affairs, Jeremy Hanley, in Beijing. The negotiations apparently had been stalled because the Chinese side balked at giving Patten a role. Of course, it was inconceivable to the British that their last governor would not take part in the celebrations marking the historic end of their rule. The British still plan to hold their own nostalgia-drenched tattoo at East Tamar, formerly the site of the naval base. Appropriately, it will be at dusk. After a simple though "grand, solemn, dignified and fitting to the historical importance of the event" ceremony in the foyer of the new Hong Kong Convention and Exhibition Centre annex, the governor will board the Royal Yacht *Britannia* and sail away.

*     *     *     *

October is the time of the year when people in Hong Kong show their true colors. On China's National Day, out come the red-and-yellow flags of the People's Republic of China. They usually grace the entrances to the Bank of China and its various branches and subsidiaries in the colony and could sometimes be seen in Kennedy Town with its fishermen's associations subsidized by Beijing. Ten days later those who sympathize with Taiwan, or at least the old Nationalist cause, break out their banners. It isn't just Rennie's Mill, which closed last July, that is bedecked with the red and blue banner of the Kuomintang. Enclaves of Nationalist supporters reside all over. They are especially strong where I live on the south side of Hong Kong. Large flags were planted every ten meters on the bridge leading to the island of Ap Lei Chau. In recent years it has often seemed the flag of the ROC (the Nationalist Republic of China) vastly outnumbered those of the PRC, as if to underscore that, the next time the Double Ten rolls around, it won't be so visible. "We believe this is the last time we can publicly display Taiwan's flag," said Tai Sik-kwan, who, along with sympathizers, draped a huge banner on top of Hong Kong's tallest peak. It was taken down a few days later. Indeed, it seems that most of the flags were lowered rather quickly this year. As I remember, last year, the flags on Ap Lei Chau bridge flew for most of October.

A few days after Patten's speech, I attended one of those commemorations whose continuing observances next year and the years thereafter the governor says will be a sign that Hong Kong remains free. A fair portion of Taiwan's community in Hong Kong gathered in a ballroom of the luxurious Regent Hotel in Kowloon to celebrate. The walls were draped with ROC flags and portraits of the patron saint of Republican China, Dr. Sun Yat-sen. These functions are normally held in a private ballroom, although two years ago the local Kuomintang backers scored a coup in their never-ending quest for official recognition by renting a government venue. Xinhua complained, and last year celebrations returned to a rented hotel ballroom. The question everybody was asking, of course, was whether these gatherings will be permitted this time next year. "Probably they'll just take down the flags and change the name to the 86th anniversary of the revolution," said Yau Shing-mu of the *Hong Kong Economic Times*. "The Chinese are very practical people."

A sizable Taiwanese community has always lived in Hong Kong. Initially, refugees from China's civil war, they flooded into the colony after the communist victory in 1949. Lately they have been joined by businessmen who, like most other expatriates, are here because of the opportunities to do business with the mainland. An estimated 20,000 Taiwan passport holders reside in Hong Kong, almost as many as Americans or British subjects. Lacking any formal diplomatic relations with Britain, Taiwan's interests are represented through a network of officials disguised as travel agents, cultural attachés, or trade services advisors. About nine different offices are headed by the Chung Hwa Travel Service, which issues travel documents and visas and serves as Taiwan's *de facto* consulate. It usually is headed by a director appointed by the foreign ministry in Taipei, who is, for all practical purposes, Taiwan's ambassador.

Taipei has been reshuffling some of its outposts and adapting in other ways in anticipation of a new climate, post-1997. Red plum blossoms were recently painted over the flag on the tail of China Airline planes that fly into Hong Kong and Macau. The name of the government information organ was also changed from the *Free*

*China Review* to the less offensive *Kwang Hwa,* which means
"Glorious China". If Taiwan's legislature ever gets around to
passing the Hong Kong and Macau Relations Act, supposed to
regulate dealings here, most of the activities will come under the
direction of the Mainland Affairs Office, which manages Taiwan's
delicate relations with the mainland.

The 2,000 or so Taiwan companies with offices in Hong Kong
have also been making their own adjustments. Like many of the
British counterparts, some have moved their legal domiciles off-
shore to protect them from any move to confiscate or nationalize
them. It is doubtful that China would do so. Beijing keenly
appreciates Taiwan's presence in Hong Kong. The colony is an
indispensable channel for the multi-billion-dollar flow of capital,
goods and tourists from Taiwan, as well as an outlet for products
made in China in Taiwan-owned factories. Mindful of this, Beijing
has adopted what appears to be a fairly tolerant attitude toward
Taipei's continued presence. Except in matters of symbolism, it
should be business as usual. The existing unofficial organization
will be allowed to continue, said Foreign Minister Qian Qichen
recently, listing six "taboos", most having to do with political
activities or using the term "Republic of China". Difficulties in
fleshing out the details of these general principles arose because the
talks between China and Taiwan have been suspended since President Lee Teng-hui visited the United States in 1995.

\*       \*       \*       \*

Hong Kong has worked itself into a patriotic fervor over a small
group of tiny islands in the East China Sea claimed by China and
Japan and called the Diaoyus by the Chinese and the Senkakus by
the Japanese. The protests have been led mainly by the Democrats
and fanned by an extraordinary burst of jingoism in the Hong
Kong media, including the English-language press. One man who
did much of the fanning was Democratic Party legislator Tsang
Kin-shing. He led the expedition of Hong Kong protesters to the

Diaoyu Islands the week before the celebration at the Regent Hotel, where he was the man of the hour. People were constantly coming up to him and saying, "You are a hero to me," or asking to have their picture taken with him. I introduced myself, and he apologized for not being able to speak English very well. Tsang is unprepossessing, fairly short, with a funny, thin mustache. He usually wears a plaid shirt, and, reputedly, spends more time on the demonstration line than legislating. He is a curious new kind of hero for Hong Kong, which up to now has had as role models only the super rich, or movie stars like Jackie Chan. Tsang would never have come to prominence without the democratic reforms that Patten proposed in 1992. A steel contractor (though he claims to have gambled most of his earnings), he was elected to a district board in 1991 and in 1995 entered Legco from one of Patten's new functional constituencies. But his main interest seems to be in leading protests, most of them, until the Diaoyu matter arose, directed against China.

The leadership of the Democratic Party doesn't quite know what to make of Tsang. His strong advocacy of increasing public spending for the less-advantaged underscores an argument that their pro-business opponents often make against them, namely that expanding democracy will lead to a welfare state, sapping the economic strength of the colony. His latest exploit, leading a small band of protesters that charged illegally into the Japanese consulate here—not for nothing is he known as "The Bull"—must have appalled people, like Martin Lee, who continually insist on the importance of maintaining the rule of law. They put a lot of pressure on him to make a public apology, which he did, sort of, insisting, in my hearing anyway, that he regretted only the minor injury to the consulate doorkeeper, not trespassing on consular property.

The Bull seems to fit a psychological need that many Hong Kong people have for heroes in this last summer as a British colony. That could be seen in the adulation of wind-surfer San San after she won Hong Kong's one and only gold medal in its history at the Atlanta Olympic Games. Hong Kong politician David Chan became a martyr this month when he drowned after jumping into waters off the Diaoyu Islands. Hong Kong people have been pushed around a lot lately, first by the British and then by China. People have demonstrated over and over to no avail against Beijing's plans for scrapping the democratically elected Legco and replacing it with a provisional one. Now by wrapping the [Chinese] flag around them, these new heroes tap into a genuinely popular cause, but also one to which China cannot readily say no. And in the year when one group of Chinese was lobbing ballistic missiles at another in the Taiwan Strait, it would be hard to overestimate the emotional impact emanating from the picture of the two antagonistic banners, one of China, the other of Taiwan, planted side-by-side on the disputed islands.

MISSION ACCOMPLISHED—*South China Morning Post*

Many expatriates in Hong Kong were taken aback, to say the least, by this burst of Chinese patriotism and by the media frenzy that accompanied it. When the protesters managed to slip past the Japanese Coast Guard and plant those Chinese and Taiwanese flags on one of the islands, the *Post*'s picture of it took up the entire front page. The rest of the English and, of course, most of the Chinese press reported the expedition in equally jingoistic terms. *Ming Pao* rhapsodized: "The imperishable noble spirit of the Chinese remain on the Diaoyu forever." *The Oriental Daily News:* "The heroic sons and daughters of China have put a new glow on the Chinese spirit." It sounded like the most epochal landing since the invasion of Normandy. "Newspapers *do* fall prey to excitement," declared Jonathan Fenby, the *Post* editor, somewhat sheepishly when he later discussed his newspaper's coverage with an audience of journalists at the Foreign Correspondents' Club. He correctly noted, I think, that sub-currents were at work, especially fears that Hong Kong citizens have that they might not be able to demonstrate for causes after 1997. "Some stories just hit a nerve that editors don't anticipate."

Some took this extraordinary coverage as conclusive proof that the good old *SCMP,* for years the organ of the British establishment, was moving wholesale into Beijing's camp. That has been talked about ever since Rupert Murdoch sold it to the supposedly old-China-friend Malaysian businessman Robert Kuok. Never mind that inflaming the Diaoyu issue was not Beijing's line this month. Indeed, the real mouthpieces, the *Ta Kung Pao* and *Wen Wei Po,* had relatively little to say editorially about the Diaoyus in tune with Beijing's desire to play the issue down in order not to antagonize relations with Japan. What is happening is something different, I think. The *Post* is repositioning itself, to be sure, but not as a pro-Beijing mouthpiece. As Hong Kong joins China, it is inevitable that its media—English as well as Chinese—will take on a more nationalistic perspective. That means it will cheer China's and Hong Kong's sports teams at international events and probably support China's fundamental interests globally, including its territorial claims in the East and South China Seas. The expatriates were perplexed because they always thought of the *Post* as being "their" newspaper. The editors want to make it Hong Kong's paper.

\*    \*    \*    \*

Foreign Minister Qian Qichen's interview in the *Asian Wall Street Journal* this month has caused considerable anxiety in local press circles. When the subject turned to press freedom after China resumes sovereignty, he said, "They [journalists] can put forward criticism, but not rumors or lies. Nor can they put forward personal attacks on Chinese leaders." The remarks was similar to the one that Lu Ping made last May when he said that advocating independence for Taiwan (or for Hong Kong and Tibet, for that matter) would not be tolerated.

It's hard to know whether such remarks are a calculated attempt to intimidate Hong Kong's media, or simply the musings of Communist Party *apparatchiks* groping in their own limited way to define freedom of the press—of which they have no experience whatsoever—in response to direct questions from Western journalists. I had felt that way about Lu's remarks. After all, he is practically a cabinet member. It would be politically incorrect, to say the least, for him to have said anything that suggested that it is okay to advocate independence for Taiwan. Qian had an opportunity, however, to modify his remarks during voting for members of the Selection Committee, and he pretty much stuck by them. "I don't regard creating rumors or making personal attacks as a type of press freedom." He also rather pointedly reminded people that Hong Kong has yet to pass laws banning subversion, treason and other acts against the state, including stealing of "state secrets", which in China are rather loosely defined. A Chinese reporter, Xi Yang, working for the Chinese-language newspaper *Ming Pao,* is serving a 12-year prison sentence for stealing "state secrets", defined in that case as bank interest rates and gold reserve policies. Many in Hong Kong felt that this was a clear shot across Hong Kong's bow warning reporters not to get too inquisitive about China's affairs.

Mak Yin-ting, chairwoman of the Hong Kong Journalists Association, got Qian's message loud and clear. "It's a way of China setting the ground rules. They're telling us that certain things, like independence for Taiwan or Tibet, are taboo," she said, when I talked with her about it later.

"Qian says we can't make personal attacks or tell lies, but what is a personal attack? His admonition is vague. And newspapers do make mistakes. Look at that British newspaper that recently was taken in by the hoax over nude pictures of Princess Diana."

In some ways, the Chinese don't have to worry about setting limits; local proprietors and editors will do it for them. Many newspaper owners have commercial interests or publishing ambitions on the mainland that they want to protect, and they may not want to publish anything that might irritate the Chinese leadership. It is often said that Rupert Murdoch pulled the BBC World Service from his Star television network in order not to undermine future business opportunities in China, for example.

The saga of another newspaper mogul is instructive. Jimmy Lai started out in the garment business and then went into publishing by launching a magazine called *Next.* After he called Premier Li Peng a "son of a turtle egg" in its pages, (Qian may have had this in mind when he talked about personal attacks) his stores in Beijing were closed. Undaunted, Lai sold his garment businesses and threw all of his resources and his considerable energy into publishing. He launched the mass circulation *Apple Daily*, which overnight became the second-largest circulating Chinese language newspaper in Hong Kong. But *Apple's* reporters are still barred from entering China on reporting assignments, even to cover such vital news to Hong Kong as meetings of the Preparatory Committee.

Journalists continually argue the extent to which self-censorship is even now being practiced. That it happens is considered self-evident—the Journalists Association surveyed members and found that 90 percent believed that it occurred either frequently or occasionally. Yet it is difficult to actually come up with specific examples. Of course, it is always hard to tell if self-censorship is under way. A lot of reasons can be given for not running a particular story. Broadcasters have been accused of not showing documentaries that have been attacked by Beijing as "anti-China". One such was *Return to the Dying Rooms,* a powerful British program about execrable conditions in Chinese orphanages. Yet many newspapers carried Amnesty International's investigations of orphanage conditions. "I can't see the situation getting any better in the future," says Mak.

The left-wing editor, Tsang Tak-sing, makes a case, not very convincingly, that 1997 actually will bring more press freedom to Hong Kong. It should be remembered that Tsang is the same person who was jailed for a couple years for distributing anti-British tracts in the playground, so one might expect that he takes a somewhat jaundiced view of free speech under the colonials. It seems that his mind is stuck back in the sixties. He will speak of an incident in which an editor at a Chinese publication was fired for publishing a disparaging remark about Princess Margaret, for example. That may well be accurate, but it is a little out of date. It is, of course, true that the past held a number of press restrictions. Colonial authorities used to ban films that they felt might roil relations with China. Back in the days when cinemas showed newsreels, they had to be purchased exclusively from British sources. At one time the top managers at the government radio stations had to be British, and so on. Many of these older laws were repealed or modified in the 1980s, although some time-bombs remain on the books, such as the Official Secrets Act. The Journalists Association had long advocated that it be repealed or modified, so far without much success.

No exodus of publications can be traced to the impending handover. Of course, local newspapers have no choice but to stay where their market is. Some of the more specialized China-watching sheets may want to do their China-watching from some other perch. Lee Yee, publisher of the *Nineties,* has reportedly made plans to relocate to Taiwan, where he already publishes a local edition. It was rumored that the *Hong Kong Economic Journal,* perhaps the most respected Chinese-language business daily (and an open supporter of Patten's political reforms) might shut down, although publisher Lam Sham-muk denies it.

For the most part, Western media are loath to lose what has been such an advantageous base. And far from abandoning Hong Kong, some news organizations have actually been boosting their presence. Some like the *Washington Post,* which had abandoned Hong Kong for Beijing when China opened in the 1980s, have reopened local bureaus. Obviously, the handover is a big draw, but Hong Kong is also an attractive place from which to cover the rest of Southeast Asia. *Time* is also enlarging its Hong Kong staff. The British news service, Reuters, however, recently announced plans to move its Asian headquarters to Singapore, known for its own tight controls on the foreign media. I understand that the decision was made in part because of concerns about trying to report objectively on Taiwan from Hong Kong and, to a lesser degree, Tibet. Other considerations may explain the moves. Office rents are beginning to rise again, and Singapore, anxious to turn itself into a regional media center, may have offered some attractive incentives.

I asked Mak if she had ever considered quitting journalism because of the dangers that might lurk beyond the handover. After all, being a reporter in Hong Kong doesn't seem to be such a wise career choice these days.

"No," she replied. "I've never been tempted to quit just because of the possible loss of press freedom, although I have considered it for other reasons," as have many other Chinese journalists. The wages are low and the hours long compared with many other opportunities for educated young people.

"I treasure the freedoms I have in Hong Kong, and I want to stay and fight for them." Brave words.

# November 1996

*"We have no favorite."*

IN A NOISY, CROWDED RESTAURANT in Kowloon, more than 1,000 graduates of Pui Kiu Middle School gather to celebrate their alma mater's fiftieth anniversary one evening in mid-November. Retired school teachers, Bank of China employees and deputy directors of Xinhua shake hands with Principal Tsang Yok-sing, sign the red memorial banner and go looking for their tables in the huge banquet hall. Tsang, who has more on his mind tonight than greeting old students, darts about nervously. The school is expecting four special guests: they are the men who hope to become Hong Kong's first post-1997 chief executive.

Only a ripple of excitement runs through the jam of news people as Lo Tak-shing enters the room. Big and rumpled, he seems to swallow the diminutive Tsang when he envelops him in a bear hug. But Lo lost much of his news currency after he dropped out of the race for chief executive a few weeks ago. Minutes later a greater stir greets the suave business tycoon, Peter Woo. He's large, too, but immaculately dressed, with a fixed smile and narrow eyes that look out like laser beams. He drapes an arm around Tsang for the photographers and heads for a side room. Moments later Tung Chee-hwa enters. Pandemonium. A dozen microphones compete for space in front of his lips, which are curled in a smile as he plows steadily through the throng to a reception room. He meets and shakes hands with Peter Woo as photographers throw themselves into another frenzy. The last guest is Simon Li, a courtly former judge who seems overwhelmed by the mob of reporters. He looks distressed, his glasses knocked askew, as friends form a protective cordon and elbow their way past reporters into the dining room. Li sits down at the head table, where he is soon joined by Tung and

Woo. (Another candidate, former Chief Justice Yang Ti-liang, had come earlier and left before dinner).

These men, three of them multi-millionaires and none an alumnus, have literally come to pay court—to the alumni of the school, one of Hong Kong's traditional left-wing institutions, but especially to Tsang Yok-sing. For Tsang also heads the Democratic Alliance for the Betterment of Hong Kong, the largest "pro-Beijing" political grouping. As such, he is in a position to influence 43 votes in the 400-member electoral college that will choose Hong Kong's first Chinese governor. A crucial test, the meeting to formally nominate candidates, is only three days away. Tsang may be physically small, but he has enormous political stature.

The election is beginning to take on the trappings of a real campaign. Like many things "Made in Hong Kong", it has the appearance of being copied from the West. It really got started on October 1, when Peter Woo declared his intention to seek the position. That in itself wasn't so remarkable. As the former boss of blue-chip corporations and currently the head of the local Hospital Authority, Woo has obvious credentials. What was unusual was the manner in which he made his political debut. In a crowded hotel ballroom facing a battery of television cameras and reporters, he issued a thoughtful campaign manifesto. Woo answered questions from the reporters in a manner that bespoke thorough prepping by handlers beforehand. It was almost as though he were announcing his intention to run for, well, president of the United States.

Ever since he announced his candidacy, Woo has seen his life change dramatically. When he arrives at his office in the morning these days, it is not the latest stock market quotes for Wharf and Wheelock, conglomerates his family controls, that draw his attention. More likely, he studies the current public opinion polls. Next on the day's agenda is a board meeting. But he will not be hearing the deferential voices he's accustomed at Wharf. No, today it is a joint meeting of the Central and Western District Boards. There, Democratic Party councillor Kam Nai-wai publicly berates him for wanting to roll back the territory's democratization. In his manifesto, Woo has proposed reintroducing some appointed seats to these local governing bodies. Everywhere he turns, a forest of microphones is thrust into his face. Wang Xizhe, the Chinese dissident, recently fled China through Hong Kong to the United States. What would he do if something like that happened after he became chief executive? "This is a question to be answered after July 1, 1997," he replies cautiously. He even launched an Internet web site with an image showing Woo against the backdrop of a futuristic Hong Kong cityscape. It included his biography, quotes, press releases and an invitation to communicate via email. He began holding daily tea receptions for the media to discuss his policy platform with reporters and talk about his family.

Once Woo set the "open and friendly" tone—despite his reputation as cold and imperious in private—the other candidates had to do the same. They too have delivered speeches, given interviews, appeared on radio call-in programs. They have opened campaign offices, hired image consultants, issued position papers. The latest polls measuring their public popularity appear regularly in the newspapers, which have given the race saturation coverage. They are followed everywhere by reporters, demanding their opinions on everything from the jailing of Chinese dissidents to whether women would be allowed to inherit property in the New Territories after the handover. When Yang Ti-liang resigned as chief justice, he had to give up his official car and 6,000-square-foot mansion on the Peak. He invited reporters to watch him move into his new digs in the luxurious Parkview apartments. "It's a bit small," he remarked artlessly, evidently not aware that his 900-square-foot apartment was considerably larger than most Hong Kong people's homes. He also was photographed hanging onto a subway strap, no doubt the first time in years he had used public transportation. The candidates have visited so many public housing estates and slums that local reporters have come to call it the "squatter beat". For many of the candidates, it must have been a revelation. When Yang visited the Elderly Rights League at its dingy headquarters in

Sham Shui Po, he was late for the meeting. He and his driver got lost, never having been to this working-class district. (Perhaps he should have stuck with his subway gig; the league is only half a block from an exit.)

Every now and then, it is necessary to remind oneself that this not a real general election. The actual decision will made by the 400 members of an electoral college called the Selection Committee, not by the colony's six million people. The election—or selection— of the first chief is thus more like that of a pope than a president, although this college of red cardinals, (well at least reds) will do their voting in public. In this instance Xinhua seems to have dropped its usual penchant for secrecy and decided to televise the proceedings. The announcement of the names of the selectors brought some interesting anomalies. Solicitor Ambrose Lau, whose Hong Kong Progressive Party (a grouping of generally pro-Beijing businessmen) has only two seats in Legco, wound up with the largest bloc of votes, 47. Little wonder that all four candidates showed up at the group's annual dinner. A Chinese newspaper photographer captured the arresting scene, all four candidates hand-in-hand with a beaming Ambrose Lau in the middle. The 400 are divided into four groups: business, professional, political and "grassroots". That is supposed to show that the committee broadly represents Hong Kong. Actually, it has a heavy bias toward business and members of generally pro-Beijing, and left-wing, political parties and trade unions. Many chuckled about the listing of Hari Harilela, patriarch of a wealthy local Indian clan which among other things owns the Holiday Inn hotel, as a "grassroots" selector. Infrastructure mogul Gordon Wu appears under the "political category", although he holds no office known to me. Both Tsang brothers are on the committee, including Tak-shing, who edits *Ta Kung Pao* and thus may be the only working journalist named.

The Democratic Party decided to boycott these proceedings, and is running its own candidate, veteran pro-democracy campaigner Szeto Wah, for chief in a mock election. The other day, as I was heading for the bus in Causeway Bay to go home, he stood alongside a life-sized cardboard cutout of himself. Next to it he was haranguing people passing by the busy intersection. Quite a few people were signing his petitions. (eventually Szeto would get about 100,000 "votes"). No Democrats may be serving as selectors, but liberal Frederick Fung was chosen, even though he was the only member of the Preparatory Committee to vote against the establishment of the provisional legislature last March, a move that many at the time thought would kill his chances of serving on the electoral college.

\*　　\*　　\*　　\*

The Selection Committee met for the first time on November 15 in a large conference room of the Hong Kong Convention and Exhibition Centre to nominate candidates. I was immediately struck by the sheer Chineseness of the setting. Everything was printed in Chinese characters. No English translation appeared anywhere, not even on the signs pointing to the location of the meeting. To enter the press section required passing through a gauntlet of grim Chinese security guards in civilian clothes—fair enough I suppose, since Foreign Minister Qian Qichen had flown into Hong Kong to preside in his role as chairman of the Preparatory Committee. A row of booths provided translation kits, but I soon found that they were for the delegates, not the press. We were on our own. Of course, Chinese ideograms would not be seen at an American presidential nomination convention, or at the Labour Party summer conference in Blackpool, either. But it was still a little spooky for someone used to bilingual signs everywhere in this officially English-speaking colony. It was as if to say, "This is our affair. You foreign journalists are welcome to observe, but we're not going to go out of the way to help you." Perhaps it is not unrelated that the Chinese Foreign Ministry this year discontinued holding briefings in English. Inside the conference room a spotlight shone on a red velvet backdrop highlighting the seal of the

People's Republic of China. It looked and felt like Beijing's Great Hall of the People had been transplanted to the shores of Victoria Harbour.

One by one the committee members walked in, chatted with colleagues and found their places in one of the seventeen rows of tables, neatly divided into the four committee sections. When a celebrity like Li Ka-shing, movie mogul Run Run Shaw, or Stanley Ho entered, it brought a brief stir from the press section. Two questions would be answered before the committee adjourned in the afternoon: How wide was Tung's support (his nomination was a foregone conclusion) and would Peter Woo win the 50 votes needed to go to the final round of voting a month hence. Of all the candidates, it was hardest to determine where Woo's strength lay. Even Simon Li could, it was thought, count on a strong bloc of votes from New Territories interests that he inherited after Lo Tak-shing pulled out of the race. Yang has support from those members closely allied to Xinhua, many of whom are left-wingers and have strong reservations about the idea of a capitalist running Hong Kong, and from some heavyweights on the Preparatory Committee, such as vice chairman Ann Tse-kai. But Woo has always been something of a Lone Ranger in the business community. He has few if any mentors, only subordinates. Even his brother-in-law, the former legislator Helmut Sohmen, who heads the shipping side of the family business, has been conspicuously absent from his campaign. Woo had some liabilities among the small group that would do the actual voting, moreover. Some still resented how he had treated Eric Cumine, the architect of Wharf's Harbour City development. He sued Cumine for "professional negligence" for allegedly failing to maximize the floor area, which Woo claimed cost millions in lost income. Losing twice locally, Woo took the case to the Privy Council where he lost again. Nonetheless, the legal battle eventually cost Cumine, once Hong Kong's leading architect, everything. It was not something that the public at large remembered, but it was not forgotten by the professionals' section of the committee made up of lawyers, doctors, accountants—and architects.

Pretty soon the vice chairmen, led by Qian and Lu Ping, filed in and took their seats on the dais. First Qian, and then Lu Ping, began to drone through lengthy speeches in Mandarin. About half of the members of the committee, not fluent in the national language, plugged their translation kits into their ears. I got bored, drifted out of the hall, drifted back in, and then decided to go over to the Marriott Hotel where Yang had made his campaign headquarters in a small room in the hotel's business center. The television in the tiny conference room, where I squeezed in with a dozen or so other journalists, carried the voting live. We watched as the committee members dropped their bright red ballots into the box. Then one by one the votes were read and a tick placed on a large white tote board on the dais. Tung quickly passed the 50 mark; his board filled so rapidly that the proceedings were temporarily suspended as an assistant wheeled out another one. Well over half of the votes were counted before Yang secured his needed 50 nominators. Just before the voting ended, Woo went over the top too, with four more votes than the minimum. Simon Li, surprisingly, fell a few votes short and was eliminated. Yang entered the room shortly before acquiring the minimum of 50 nominators to a scattering of applause. He replied, "Thank you, thank you," and gave a short speech, saying he was delighted to be an official nominee. Meanwhile behind him the screen showed Tung steadily piling up the votes. Shortly before the balloting was concluded, he went over 200, enough by itself to win election if all stayed. I asked Yang if he felt the race was over.

"No way, no way, we have to wait until December 11. I must meet more people and refine my platform." He can meet more people and rewrite his platform endlessly and it would not stop the Tung juggernaut now.

A few days after the nominating session, Tung was introduced at the session of the World Economic Forum as Hong Kong's "forthcoming governor". Having won an absolute majority of 206 votes, his election is assured. But he still must go through the motions, as do the other candidates. Indeed, if anything, Tung is busier, even if his schedule seems to have changed subtly. Instead of, say, the Young Industrialists Council, he is concentrating on housing estates, tenement buildings, squatter villages and other working-class neighborhoods. Ostensibly, these visits are designed "to deepen his understanding of housing, education and welfare issues". Yes, but he had another purpose too. All year he has been the acknowledged front-runner, yet he had always lagged far behind in public opinion polls. As late as August, after months of intensive speculation about his candidacy, Tung barely attracted five percent in various polls (Anson Chan blew everyone away with over 50 percent.) When Chan formally pulled out of the race and was finally dropped from the polling, Yang surged to the head. Unless Tung can get his numbers up, he will be forever branded simply as China's choice, not Hong Kong's.

Which was why on a Friday in late November the candidate, dressed casually in a blue shirt open at the neck and a sweater is sitting at the front table in the dingy headquarters of the Elderly Welfare League three flights above a seed store in the crowded district of Sham Shui Po in Kowloon. Behind him a banner reads, WE DEMAND FROM THE NEW CHIEF EXECUTIVE A POLICY ON AGING. To his front the small room is crowded with elderly people sitting on folding metal chairs. They are questioning Tung about his knowledge of housing:

"How long does it take to qualify for public housing in Hong Kong?" one person asks.

"Five years," says Tung.

"Seven years," replies the man with a toothless grin

"How much does it cost to rent a cage in a tenement house?" asks another.

"Eight hundred dollars a month," he ventures.

"More like a thousand dollars," replies the questioner

After leaving the Elderly Rights League he is driven to a tenement in Mongkok to meet with a family of recent immigrants from the mainland. Meanwhile, I followed the press pack to another part of Kowloon, where the "cage men" live. We climb three flights of dirty concrete stairs into the flophouse where elderly men make their home literally in wire metal cages, stacked one on top of the other as in a dog kennel. It is designed, I suppose, to allow them to protect their possessions, such as they are. The residents seemed bewildered by this mob of press and snarl at the photographers who try to take their pictures hunkered down in their cages. After a short while, Tung and his small entourage arrive. Television camera lights throw strange shadows around the dark room. He disappears in a corner to question one of the residents, too far away for me to hear. Afterward on the sidewalk, he gives his impression to the clutch of journalists.

"It's worse than I imagined."

\*   \*   \*   \*

Opening the first session of the Selection Committee, Foreign Minister Qian Qichen said, "In the past 150 years, Britain has appointed more than 20 Hong Kong governors without consulting the local community. Only at this time do Hong Kong people have a democratic right of picking the chief executive." There is no shortage of critics to dispute that claim and brand the whole exercise a sham. Not all are from the Western media. Outside of the convention hall, while Qian was proclaiming a "new era for Hong Kong", a raucous group of Hong Kong demonstrators denounced the committee and burned a black coffin supposedly symbolizing the death of democracy. They were led by some familiar faces such as The Bull and Leung Kwok-hung. A month later, when the committee convened again actually to select Tung as the next chief, the same crew was back. This time around a dozen demonstrators, including the liberal legislator Emily Lau, were arrested as they staged a sit-down strike on the sidewalk outside the convention center. Is this a foretaste of more to come, as Democrats and other independent groups, such as Lau's Frontier, become opposition forces outside the mainstream of the political structure of the future SAR? In Legco, Leung Yiu-chung denounced the whole selection process as a fraud in a speech so incendiary—he used a Cantonese epithet, "foul grass growing out of a foul ditch", to describe the procedure—that he was thrown out of the chamber.

But it seems to me that those who are quick to dismiss this as a sham may be too cynical. In its own peculiar way an open and, shall one dare say, a kind of proto-, democracy was at work. Few could watch without being impressed as the candidates spent three days being grilled by the committee members on live television about their platforms, political philosophy and plans for Hong Kong. And it wasn't just the rich and famous on the committee who were doing all the questioning. Hundreds of ordinary people got their licks in through radio call-in programs or in smaller forums such as the one held at the Elderly Rights League. Local residents are learning a lot about the contestants, and, they—three of them multi-millionaires—in turn are learning a little about how the other half lives. Despite its obviously narrow franchise, the leadership race has put the candidates under a public microscope, exposing them to the kinds of gaffes and slip-ups that politicians in other countries with universal suffrage have learned to endure. Case in point: Simon Li may have seriously damaged his chances of getting nominated when, in response to a radio-call-in question, he revealed confidential information from the on-going Sino-British negotiations over the 1997/98 budget. It was an ill-advised bid to impress the public. He said that Beijing wanted to cut the annual rate of welfare spending from 25 percent to 20 percent.

Public opinion polls played a major role throughout the autumn campaign, and in fact through most of the year. Certainly Anson Chan's reputation as the people's choice was founded on her consistently high numbers. Conversely, Lo finally bowed out when it became clear that he did not command the popular support needed by a credible chief. The polls may not have influenced the members of the Selection Committee, but the candidates themselves understood that it would be fatal for their chances of governing effectively to be found at the bottom. Polls were no longer seen simply as an academic exercise but as a quasi-election. That's why it was so important to Tung that he also have a stamp of public approval as manifested in the only possible forum in this campaign, the polls. In one survey published on December 2, Tung did lead the other candidates with 46 percent approval versus 28 for Yang and 5.2 for Peter Woo, who despite the slickness of his campaign, or perhaps because of it, never seemed to be able to get his own numbers up much higher than single digits.

On December 11, the man that President Jiang shook hands with so publicly nearly a year ago receives 320 votes and thus becomes Hong Kong's new chief executive–elect. Should one be surprised? "If the Chinese Communist Party does not have a predetermined winner in an election, that is not the Communist Party," said Democratic Party whip Szeto Wah. That, of course, begs the question about why other candidates, people like Woo, chief justice Yang, or Lo Tak-shing, were so willing to be the secondary players in a production entirely scripted in Beijing. Lo had bank-rolled *Window* though four money-losing years before he finally folded the publication three weeks after his friend, Simon Li, failed to get nominated. It was no longer necessary. Lo tried to position himself as the most assertively pro-Beijing candidate in the field, but he never caught on among any significant sector of the community and pulled out. His surrogate also failed.

The election of the first chief executive is a major public relations success for Beijing, after a number of fumbles earlier this year. It is not so much that they managed to put their own man in office. Rather, the process was widely seen as conferring a kind of legitimacy that the winner will find invaluable in the delicate task of governing Hong Kong in the critical early years following the transition. President Jiang Zemin played a part in this when, earlier this year, he stated publicly that the new chief executive must be acceptable to the people of Hong Kong. Qian Qichen made overtures to the Democrats to join the process; later he stressed several times, including in his welcoming speech to the Selection

Committee, that Beijing did not have its own candidate: "We have no favorite."

It seems to me that those who criticize Tung as being too close to China are searching for a Chinese version of Chris Patten, a kind of Hong Kong tribune. It is not entirely clear that this would be the best choice for Hong Kong, and, in any case, the system was never likely to provide one. Essentially, it was designed to produce a future ruler who was broadly acceptable to both the leadership in Beijing and the Hong Kong community. "China has a constitutional interest and right to make sure that all the candidates are reasonably acceptable," said legislator David Chu, as we discussed the results over breakfast one morning. "They make the final appointment, after the Selection Committee makes its recommendation. Theirs is not a rubber stamp; it's a real stamp."

In time, the selection of Hong Kong's chief executive could evolve into something seriously approaching a real election. The Basic Law holds out the tantalizing possibility of electing the chief executive through universal suffrage after 2007. Although he will be constitutionally barred from running after two five-year terms, it is not hard to imagine Tung doing reasonably well in an open electoral process. True, his poll numbers were low through most of the year, but they began rising steadily after he openly declared for the job (while Lo could barely muster one percent even after he declared). Tung has an empathy with people that seems to come through in his interactions with the public, and he never seemed to put a wrong foot forward during the campaign. At 67 it is hard to imagine that Yang would make another try for the job. But he can, if nothing else, look back to participating as a main character in an important historical event. Which is more than most judges can say when they retire from the bench. The last is clearly not heard from Peter Woo, whom some think used this race as a warm-up for a future when the franchise may be much broader and where his professionalism and obvious media skills will be better served than in the small, clubby atmosphere of the Selection Committee.

Four local citizens have stood up and enunciated their visions for the community's next incarnation. All have made earnest attempts to address a range of issues: What values do we deem important? What kind of relationship should we have with China? Indeed, the debate on such questions will continue long after 1997, for it is not something that China can readily stop. It is through such a process of psychological decolonization that Hong Kong will ultimately find the identity, self-confidence and political maturity it needs not only to survive but to thrive in the new era that begins next summer.

# January 1997

*"The feel-good factor has returned."*

F OR YEARS, 1997 was just the name of a night club. Or a number on a T-shirt that tourists bought at the Star Ferry, usually showing a figure covering the British flag with red paint. Or, again, it was a personalized license plate: HKI997 was traded on the secondary market for ever increasing millions of Hong Kong dollars, although the plate did not have quite the market value as one issued nine years earlier. (But then the numerals 88 have a specially happy meaning in Cantonese, the numerals *bat, bat,* rhyming with *fat* which means prosperity.) For most people, the number 97 offers nothing but a sense of foreboding.

Now that the fateful year has arrived, nevertheless, people seem to be in an unexpectedly buoyant mood. "The feel-good factor has returned," wrote the *South China Morning Post.* Most of the usual indicators of confidence are positive. The stock market is at an all-time high, having surged steadily though most of 1996. The property market is showing renewed exuberance. Inflation has abated and unemployment is practically nonexistent. Emigration has dropped to the lowest level since just before the Tiananmen massacre. Public opinion polls show that confidence in the future is high—perhaps most of the pessimists have already emigrated. The *Asian Wall Street Journal* publishes a monthly table of confidence indicators that is now often in stark contrast to the generally gloomy assessments on the editorial pages.

Lunching with some friends at the Kowloon Cricket Club, I noticed long lines of anxious buyers lining up for chances to purchase 291 luxury apartments in Sun Hung Kai's new King's Park Villa project across the street. In recent years, as prosperity spread faster than the availability of land, hundreds of people have stood in long lines for the chance to buy, and, just as often, quickly to resell, new apartment buildings. Two years ago, during the last speculative binge, the government introduced a new lottery scheme to try to bring some order to the property market and to dampen rampant speculation. So now people line up by the hundreds in order to win the chance to buy new apartments; these chances, or buying rights, are quickly resold at ever higher prices. Hovering around them like locusts are real estate agents anxious to scoop them up. Some of the premium spots in the line reportedly are going for hundreds of thousands of us dollars. No doubt about it, in these final months of British rule, property speculation is back with a vengeance.

Most of the action, however, has been in the upper end of the market. Luxury homes on the Peak bring record sums. One mountain-top mansion reportedly sold for us$70 million. Prices for middle-class apartments have not moved so much. For some this suggests a more sinister side-effect of the property boom. Savvy Hongkongers are buying apartments in anticipation of unloading them on the well-heeled rubes from the Chinese mainland, who, many believe, will be pouring into the territory after July 1. It may be that they anticipate selling at "friendship" prices, in other words, offering subtle bribes to the mainlanders. While general confidence in the future is high, those who believe corruption will also increase is growing. The Hong Kong Transition Project, which has been tracing public opinion for several years, sees a marked increase in the number of people concerned about corruption. About 30 percent say they are "very concerned". "That's the highest we've ever had," said project director Michael DeGolyer. Meanwhile, concern over stability and personal freedoms seems to be abating.

When people aren't talking about property, it seems that their attention has been diverted by another subject, and it isn't the impending handover. When Tung Chee-hwa's popularity took a dive because of his conservative stance on repealing parts of the Bill of Rights, *Apple Daily* buried the story. Prominently displayed on the front page was the latest episode in the month-long running real-life soap opera of the Tang clan. It is a perfect Hong Kong *Dynasty* involving a rich Cantonese opera star, his younger girl-friend-turned-wife, their grasping children, plus a sprinkling of sex, triads, and even allegations of opium smoking. Tang Wing-cheung lies ill in a hospital while his children and wife fight over the future division of his fortune. The saga dominated the news during much of December and January, the time that the election for chief executive was under way. The press contingent on per-manent watch around Tang's home was certainly as large as that staking out Tung's. Then on Pamela Pak's talk show, the wife's colorful brother-in-law, known as "Uncle Eight" presumably from his birth order in the family, made some startling revelations about Tang's relationship with his daughter as well as a number of other inflammatory, though unsubstantiated, assertions. The station manager ordered the show halted in mid-stream, and suspended Pak and her co-host. The story seems to have petered out for the moment, though it stands to be revived soon as the libel suits hit the courts.

*       *       *       *

Tung says he doesn't want to be known as chief executive-*designate* any more. As far as he's concerned, he's got the job and is busy putting together the first SAR government and behaving as if he were already Hong Kong's boss. The selection of the provisional legislature members in late December adds to the feeling that Hong Kong now has two parallel governments in action. While the selection of the new chief executive had a certain dignity, the same could not be said of the polling for the provisional legislature. In this case, it involved no campaign banners, no election forums, no public opinion polls. It was an unseemly I'll-vote-for-you-if-you-vote-for-me scramble that Patten, with some justification, said made his stomach churn to watch. Of the 60 members, 51 were serving on the Selection Committee, and 33 are members of the current Legco. Ten had run in the last legislative election and lost.

One Democratic Party district board member, Dominic Chan, was appointed and promptly expelled from the party for breaking discipline. Frederick Fung of the moderate Alliance for Democracy and People's Livelihood was also chosen, despite his voting against the provisional legislature last March. Poor Samuel Wong, the "engineering a better Hong Kong" man, lost, becoming the only Legco member to apply for the provisional legislature and lose. The height of grasping ambition was demonstrated by Andrew Wong, presiding officer of Legco, who not only sought and got membership in the provisional body but tried to become its presiding officer too. He was defeated by Rita Fan, a former executive councillor. He just survived a Legco vote of no confidence, filed by Democratic Party members already upset that he was being perhaps too helpful to the other body, as in passing a copy of Legco's standing orders to it.

So Hong Kong is in the curious position of having two legislatures, composed to a large degree of the same people, meeting in separate cities, working on different agendas. The provisionals have to meet for the time being across the border in Shenzhen because Patten views the body as illegitimate and has ordained non-cooperation. It has a busy agenda. Some decisions, such as appointments to the new Court of Final Appeal and review of the 1997/98 budget, must be ready for approval by Tung on July 1. More controversial is the task of devising new electoral rules to replace Patten's political reforms. Another is to define what is meant by "treason, sedition, secession and subversion" in Article 23, that time bomb ticking away in the Basic Law. This is such a touchy subject that many would like the legislature to postpone action until the election of the first SAR legislature under more democratic procedures.

But, I must say, the leaders of the three main parties had a very civilized discussion about the whole thing on Frank Ching's Sunday television talk show. If Martin Lee was upset about the situation, he didn't show much passion. He and Tsang Yok-sing and Allen Lee, leader of the Liberal Party, discussed the modalities of the two legislatures, as if they were discussing the arrangement for a cricket match. They made for a fascinating tableau. There was Martin Lee, an elected member of Legco, soon to lose his seat. There was Tsang of the DAB, who ran for Legco in 1995 and lost (I distinctly remember him saying he would not serve on the provisional legislature if he lost), and finally Allen Lee, a member of both bodies. ("Mrs. Chan, please check my diary. Am I supposed to be in Hong Kong or Shenzhen today?")

Everybody agrees that the sooner the provisional body does its work and disbands, the better. Tung has promised to try to get through the business in a year or less, allowing for new elections in mid-1998. That may not be soon enough to undo the damage already done to Hong Kong in the eyes of the West. The press greeted China's plans to disband Legco with widespread and negative media coverage. In Washington, a move is apparently afoot to deny entry visas for members of the provisional body. Considerable indignation resulted as rumors of this action swept through the Shenzhen Guest House where the legislature was holding its opening session in early February. Chim Pui-chung, who is known to enjoy gambling in Las Vegas from time to time, got pretty worked up about it. "If they ban us, the provisional legislature will pass a bill banning members of the US Senate" from Hong Kong, he thundered. It is very unlikely that the situation would reach such an impasse. Still, Congress is beginning to build up a head of steam over the disquieting events here over the past few months. Unfortunately, the nuances and details of the transition tend to get lost in the transmission. By the time the story reaches the congressman's breakfast table, it boils down to simple verities, namely that in Hong Kong, China is extinguishing democracy forever. One Washington power broker told a colleague of mine, "You better get out of there by July 1; China is going to ruin the place." The impressions are reinforced by Patten, who is widely respected in the West but who is also very partisan and articulate in defending his own political reforms and predicting the dire consequences that will come from dismantling them. Those Hong

Kong people with a different point of view, such as Allen Lee, often get snubbed.

*    *    *    *

The provisional legislature had hardly held its first meeting before another political bomb exploded in Beijing. The legal subcommittee of the Preparatory Committee finished scrutinizing all 550 local ordinances and recommended that about two dozen of them be either scrapped or modified because they conflict with the Basic Law or are politically unacceptable to Beijing. The action has caused considerable disquiet in the territory and gave the impression abroad that Beijing is intent not only on snuffing out democracy through the provisional legislature, but also systematically eliminating Hong Kong's traditional liberties. Chief Secretary Anson Chan returned from a trip to the US complaining that the recommendations had sent an extremely negative signal. "Of course, I took this opportunity to try to put forward a positive side of Hong Kong," Chan said of her trip, "but I must confess that the latest development has made my job rather more difficult."

Many of the statutes that the committee wants to junk have little to do with civil liberties. Some are anachronisms, such as the "Colony Armorial Bearings (Protection) Ordinance", which prohibits the use of Hong Kong's royal coat of arms without permission. The real controversy centers on the proposal to reinstate certain sections of the Societies Ordinance and the Public Order Ordinance that were scrapped by the government in 1992 and 1995 respectively. The former limits the freedom of local political groups to form links with foreign organizations (and clearly harked back to the days immediately following the Chinese civil war when these "links" were understood to be either with the Chinese Communist Party or its bitter rival the Kuomintang on Taiwan). The other required police permission for public demonstrations. As amended, only notification is required. The committee also recommended modifying certain aspects of the Bill of Rights, adopted in 1991, which it believes override the Basic Law.

The proposals are understandable within a Chinese context in that they impinge on Beijing's obsessions: stability, national integrity and suspicion of foreign meddling. In January, vice chairman Wang Hanbing of the National People's Congress reiterated the "five principles" that guide China on reversion. The cardinal one is that Hong Kong "will remain an autonomous, international city as far as business, finance, commerce and shipping are concerned but cannot become a base for 'anti-China' or 'anti-Communist' activity, especially any organized by foreign powers." It also says the center will take "resolute actions" in the case of "uncontrollable political riots," be they spontaneous or instigated by foreign powers. It is almost as if the leaders in Beijing think that Hong Kong is back in the 1950s when these laws were passed by a colonial administration so concerned about fighting breaking out between rival communists and Kuomintang sympathizers that they often had to segregate the two groups. Through the Cultural Revolution era, the British were always worried that local communists would stir up trouble in Hong Kong, providing Beijing with an excuse to move in and "re-establish order". The irony is that it was only after they agreed to return Hong Kong on a fixed timetable that they felt secure enough to begin repealing some of these laws.

That the Preparatory Committee was not intent on dismembering Hong Kong's civil liberties wholesale can be seen in what it chose to pass over. It did not, for example, recommend changing Democratic Party leader Martin Lee's amendment to the Film Censorship Ordinance, which removed the censor's power to ban films thought to be damaging to relations with neighboring territories (read China). Also left intact were some related to Hong Kong's constitutional development. The Legislative Council (Powers and Privileges) Ordinance gives the legislature the power to summon top government officials for open questioning on sensitive issues. The legislature wielded this with a vengeance this month when it hauled in the chief secretary to explain the reasons behind the resignation last summer of former immigration director Laurence Leung under suspicious circumstances. It may well be that the legislators were using this case to establish a firm precedent for questioning government officials after the handover. Another overturned tradition by allowing women in the rural New Territories to inherit land. In fact, nobody was angrier about the proposals than the Heung Yee Kuk, which represents the interests of traditional landowners in the New Territories and is normally a bulwark of support for the Chinese government. Their leader Lau Wong-fat stormed out of the meeting of the full committee where the vote over repealing the laws was taken.

Many in the territory felt that Tung was too quick to endorse the committee's proposals down the line, taking some of the glow off the general good will that had followed his selection a month earlier. In a speech to the "Leader of the Year" awards ceremony, Tung described them as mainly technical. "The issue is not about human rights. If people want to demonstrate or lie down the middle of the road, in my view, they should be allowed to do so. But they must do so without causing inconvenience and harm to the community at large and they must do so within the law." As for the Societies Ordinance, Tung said the issue is: "Do we want Hong Kong's political parties to have associations with foreign political parties? Could it destabilize Hong Kong? The answer must be that we should not let this happen." Even some local politicians, who often sympathize with Beijing's point of view, believe the changes are unwarranted. "I've read the Basic Law again and again, and I cannot find how it is infringed," said Allen Lee. Though the number of demonstrations has increased along with transition tensions, none has produced any violence or bloodshed. Last October some activists protesting Japanese occupation of the Diaoyu Islands barged illegally into the Japanese consulate when emotions over disputed islands in the East China Sea were running high. That was about the most radical act of civil disobedience I can remember. Rumors make the rounds of actions planned for the day of the handover, such as the Democrats chaining themselves to their Legco desks. And in the supercharged atmosphere of 1997 it should not surprise anyone that Tung might want a few more tools in his kit when he takes over. After all, it is he who will have to deal with any civil disturbances that might accompany the change of sovereignty, possibly before he has time to locate the men's room at Government House.

A few years ago, I had an opportunity to observe how one of these disputed laws worked in practice. One of the purposes of the old Societies Ordinance was to help control triads, criminal secret societies. All organizations had to register with the government; thus those belonging to an unregistered or "secret" society were automatically breaking the law regardless of whether they were committing a conventional crime. I spent the afternoon in a north Kowloon magistrate's courtroom, practically empty save for the defendant's relatives. The defendant was a small fry, nothing like a dragon-head, or some other triad leader. It wasn't even clear that 25-year-old Tam Wing-keung was a triad, merely that he had claimed to be one. It was a late colonial tableau. The presiding judge, sitting beneath the royal court of arms, was an Englishman. A British police inspector served as the prosecutor. All of the proceedings were in English, though difficult to hear from the press box, where I sat as the lone observer. The defendant had made the mistake of boasting to an off-duty policeman in a Mongkok convenience store that he was a triad. "I'm of the Sun Yee On," he had said in a fit of bravado, referring to Hong Kong's largest triad. He didn't have much of a defense, and he was ultimately fined about US$100.

This system always had a certain unfairness. Why should some-one be penalized simply for belonging to a group, rather than for committing a real crime, such as loan-sharking or extorting money? In this case, Tam had been penalized for something he said rather than something he did. In 1992 the Societies Ordinance was amended to draw a distinction between technical infringement for societies formed for innocent purposes and those formed for unlawful purposes. It also dropped the requirement for registration and substituted simple notification. Also amended was the section that prohibited local groups from maintaining direct links with foreign political organizations. The latter is clearly contrary to the Basic Law, but perhaps when the provisional legislature gets around to passing a new Societies Ordinance, it will reinstate some of the more progressive elements that were thrown out.

Every January, Hong Kong's judges, resplendent in their black and red silk gowns and white horse-hair wigs, file into the Roman Catholic Cathedral of the Immaculate Conception for the opening of the legal year. Pictures of the Chinese and European judges in their traditional get-up grace the front pages of the newspapers. (A 1995 survey of judges indicated that a large majority wanted to keep their wigs after the handover. In any event, the wigs are said to be popular with Chinese tourists. Queen's Counsels will become Senior Counsels; not quite the same cachet.) This tableau underscores just how much Hong Kong's legal system is based on the English common law. The legal profession is comprised of barristers and solicitors, almost all proceedings are in English, and accused criminals are tried by juries of their peers. The Basic Law states clearly: "The judicial system previously practiced in Hong Kong shall be maintained." So after July 1 "red" judges (from the color of their gowns not their political persuasion) will still sit on High Court benches. Barristers will still address them respectfully as "Your Lordship". But while the trappings of English justice remain, what about the substance?

This month a US District court judge in Boston refused to extradite an accused smuggler, Jerry Lui, back to Hong Kong because he would have to go on trial here after July 1. Judge Joseph Tauro apparently made his decision on the rather narrow grounds that he would be handing the man over to China, with which the US does not have a treaty at present. The Justice Department, anxious that the US not become a future haven for Hong Kong criminals, has appealed the decision. Separate extradition and prisoner-exchange treaties have been negotiated but await US Senate approval.

Over at the attorney general's office, Tony Yen and his crew of lawyers and translators are working overtime to turn into Chinese the accumulation of 150 years of British colonial rule. It's quite a challenge, translating the common law, some of the terms incomprehensible even to untrained English speakers, into the language of a country with no common law tradition, not even, some would argue, respect for the rule of law. Altogether, they've had to translate 550 ordinances, amounting to about 21,000 pages of text. They've been working at it for nearly ten years, and, Yen tells me, all of the basic translations have been completed. They are slowly working their way through a complex vetting process, about two-thirds completed and which Yen confidently expects will be finished by July 1. It hasn't been an easy job. Take a typical phrase like "the burden of proof". Says Yen, "That's not so hard. There are accepted transliterations of the main word." In literal Chinese it comes out as something like "responsibility for providing evidence". But other, more arcane, legal terms derived from Europe's feudal past have proved to be almost impossible to translate. "Sometimes we've had to coin entirely new words," he said. The results have sometimes been criticized as being inelegant Chinese, a charge not unknown to English legalese either.

A more serious concern is that disagreements will arise over different meanings between the Chinese and English. "The fear held by many is that a wholesale swing toward the use of Chinese throughout our courts will eventually lead to the abandonment of the common law system," said Law Society president Christopher Chan recently. "We anticipated this problem when we began ten years ago," responds Yen. They studied and adopted some of the solutions of other bi- and multi-lingual jurisdictions, such as Canada and the United Nations. He notes that arguments over the meanings of words are unavoidable in the courts, even in monolingual environments. Because of the complexities of the common law, the judiciary, now about half expatriate, will likely be staffed with foreigners for many years after the handover. Indeed, Attorney General Jeremy Matthews is the only senior British head of department remaining in the civil service, now "localized" with ethnic Chinese. One of the chief executive's most critical appointments will be Matthews' replacement, to be styled "secretary of justice". He or she will have to defend the government from what is anticipated to be an avalanche of lawsuits challenging, for example, the legality of the provisional legislature and any laws it passes.

All of this means that English will continue to be the primary language of Hong Kong's courts for a long time. In recent years some lower court trials have been conducted in Cantonese, but, in the higher courts, English is still the rule. Even Chinese lawyers, many trained abroad in London's Inns of Court, may feel more comfortable arguing fine points of law in English. Many of the precedents, moreover, would be taken from other common-law jurisdictions, almost invariably in English. Jury trials are still conducted in English, which raises the question whether the 98 percent Chinese majority really receive a trial by their "peers" since the jury pool is by necessity heavily weighted toward expatriates. Only about 250,000 of the territory's 6.3 million people are fluent enough to follow the proceedings in English and thus eligible to serve on juries. One of the complaints of expats living here is that they are always being hauled in for jury duty. "We're not trying to abandon the use of English entirely; we're providing an alternative," says legal draftsman Yen. "We'll still need one or two generations before we become completely bilingual."

The other major change in Hong Kong's judicial setup actually required because of the change of sovereignty is the formation of a Court of Final Appeal, to replace the Judicial Committee of the Privy Council in London as the SAR's new court of last resort. Appeals have occurred about ten times a year. The composition of the body, which takes office on July 1, was a matter of negotiation between Britain and China. It was finally agreed in 1995 that it would comprise five justices, one of whom may be a foreigner. The agreement was condemned as soon as it was announced as weakening the region's promised autonomy. Martin Lee, himself a barrister, denounced the result as "the end of the rule of law in Hong Kong," a rather sweeping statement considering that the main bone of contention is whether there should be one or two foreign judges on the panel.

Some uncertainty surrounds the exclusion of "acts of state" from the panel's purview. Some say it provides an opening for Beijing to meddle in Hong Kong affairs by claiming that some issue is outside the local courts' jurisdiction. Say somebody sues a commercial unit of the PLA for breach of contract, might the army unit argue that it can't be tried? Unfortunately, Chris Patten pointed out, the words are in the Basic Law, which says that defense and foreign affairs are the responsibility of the national government. Some would have preferred that the court go into operation a few years before the handover date so that a body of precedents on this sensitive issue might have been established while Hong Kong is still under British administration.

Despite some of the doubts raised over the appeals court, translations of laws and other legal issues, it is to the courts and not the barricades that Lee and other liberal leaders plan to go to try to undo some of the damage they feel has been done to Hong Kong's promised autonomy by recent Chinese actions. They pledge to file a flurry of law suits challenging the constitutionality of the provisional legislature and the laws it passes. That seems to suggest that, for all the activists' rhetoric, even those who are pessimistic about the future must believe that the rule of law will prevail after 1997.

# February 1997

*"It's like leaving an old friend."*

HONG KONG AWOKE on February 20 to learn that Chinese patriarch Deng Xiaoping, the man who devised the "one country, two systems" formula, the man who coined the phrase, "Hong Kong people ruling Hong Kong", had died. Some were awakened early by the insistent beeping of their pagers warning them to expect a wild day on the stock exchange. In the past, the market has reacted like a Pavlovian dog, plunging at rumors that Deng was near death, reviving again after the official denials and the evident lack of any formal funeral arrangements. This time the rumors were true, but strangely the markets did not crash. Instead, the Hang Seng Index actually rose about 300 points, its biggest gain of the year. Most of the newspapers carried special editions, usually with a full-page portrait of the man surrounded by a black border. DENG DIES, said the *Post's* headline simply. It must have taken some fancy footwork to put these special editions together. The official announcement was not made until 2:30 AM, although strong rumors of Deng's deteriorating condition had been circulating for several days.

Riding to work the next morning, I noticed fairly long lines of mourners at Xinhua's headquarters in Happy Valley, stretching across the street to the Jockey Club. The building itself was surrounded with bright orange floral wreaths, with black crepe draped across the entrance. Hong Kong tycoons such as Li Ka-shing and movie mogul Run Run Shaw all showed up at the shrine set up just inside the entrance, of course. But unexpected mourners also paid their respects, including Chris Patten and two leaders of the Democratic Party. Old-time residents, who remember the death of Mao Zedong in 1976, say that the emotions displayed for

Deng were considerably more subdued. This is probably a good sign. Much of the weeping and wailing that accompanied Mao's death must have reflected considerable nervousness about the future. Two months before Mao died, a monster earthquake leveled the large industrial city of Tangshan near Beijing, killing half a million people. Many Chinese, naturally enough, had interpreted this as a bad omen not only of Mao's impending death but of trouble to come. The earth did not move when Deng died.

The transition in Hong Kong has probably progressed too far to be very much affected by Deng's demise. After all, most of the key elements of the incoming administration are in place: the new chief executive has been selected, and he has picked his governing team. The provisional legislature is organized; the senior civil servants confirmed in their posts and even the first post-1997 budget approved by the British and Chinese negotiators. In Tung Chee-hwa, China's rulers had found a leader that they evidently trust (he was named to the 459-member funeral committee). So they will be inclined to leave Hong Kong in his hands and get on with the immensely more difficult task of running China. Still, it is too bad that the old man did not live to see the results of his handiwork.

Tung was in Beijing when the patriarch died, but he returned to Hong Kong and held a scheduled press conference to announce his choices to head the major civil service departments. He opted for continuity by reappointing virtually all of the current department heads, including Chief Secretary Anson Chan and Financial Secretary Donald Tsang. The British, who were keen to have a "through-train" on the executive side—especially after the legislative through-train was derailed—must have been pleased. Tsang, who has publicly opposed the new chief on several issues, including his stand on repealing some civil rights laws, generates much speculation. He apparently also irritated China by weighing in on the question of immediately transferring billions of dollars of land revenue funds, held in escrow by the Chinese, back to Hong Kong after the handover. The *Asia Times* said flatly that Tsang will be removed after a decent interval, but then it also said that T.S. Lo was Beijing's man to become chief executive. There was never any doubt that Tung would reappoint Anson Chan, even though, after returning from a US trip, she was mildly critical of his quick endorsement of the rollback of Hong Kong laws. But for a variety or reasons Chan is virtually untouchable. If Tung had failed to reappoint her, it would have sent tremors through the colony.

\*   \*   \*   \*

Unemployment hardly exists in Hong Kong, yet Fred Li, for one, knows that he will be out of a job at midnight June 30, when Legco, on which he serves, disbands. Like his Democratic Party colleagues and some other small-*d* democrats, he chose as a matter of principle not to join the unelected provisional legislature that replaces it. The former Baptist University lecturer is a full-time politician, so on July 1 he not only forfeits his office but also the US$7,000 per month that goes with it, his only source of income. Hong Kong politicians without a profession or independent means of support are looking forward to a lean year in many respects. Li told me that he hopes to be able to return to the classroom at least on a part-time basis, but he already has his eye on a comeback when elections for the first post-1997 legislature are held. "I'll remain as active as possible in my constituency until then."

These are difficult times for Hong Kong's democrats, a term that encompasses not only Martin Lee's Democratic Party but also other, smaller groupings such as Frederick Fung's Alliance for Democracy and People's Livelihood, Emily Lau's new Frontier and some liberal independents, such as Christine Loh, and perhaps Margaret Ng, the maverick liberal who represents the legal constituency. Together they make up half of the 60 seats in Legco. In the two elections since direct voting from geographical seats was first introduced in 1991, the democrats have trounced their opponents. Now they face a rapidly changing and increasingly challenging political environment that will seriously test the progress that has been made toward democracy in Hong Kong.

Their most immediate problem is the loss of momentum from being out of office for at least one year. They will lose their public forum, the ability to submit bills, make news, and do favors for constituents. No longer will they be able to claim a US$20,000 allowance for staff and district offices to help with the vital constituency work between elections. Some, like Fred Li, who also serve on local councils, may be able to use those offices to stay in touch with the grassroots, assuming, as is widely anticipated, that Tung reappoints all of the incumbents, including democrats, to new "provisional" councils until new selection procedures are established. The Democratic Party recently launched a drive to raise the money to try to survive the lean months ahead in the political wilderness. You can see them wearing their green vests and manning booths at busy intersections and at the entrances to the Star Ferry. Raising money among overseas Chinese in Canada and the US is also one purpose of Martin Lee's latest tour.

When new elections are held for the first post-1997 legislature, they will be under an entirely different set of rules. Twenty directly elected seats are guaranteed in the Basic Law. But dozens of legitimate ways exist to configure elections. The provisional legislature can be counted on to choose one that will put the democrats at greatest disadvantage. They have thrived in first-past-the-post elections. The Democratic Alliance for the Betterment of Hong Kong (DAB) and the Liberal Party are pushing for proportional representation. Xinhua favors a one-vote, multi-seat system, where two members are elected from each district. Either one would probably cost the democrats seats. The fear that certain prominent democrats, such as Martin Lee or Szeto Wah, might be barred from running for office, or, worse, imprisoned has receded. Either action would certainly cause China unending troubles abroad and, anyway, may not be necessary. With some deft electoral management, the democratic representation in the new Legco can be reduced to a rump. Lee himself figures that the democrats of all persuasions will be lucky to get as many as twelve seats (based on their 65 percent vote total in 1995), plus maybe two out of the 30 seats elected by special interests.

A different and cooler atmosphere will prevail at Government House (or wherever Tung decides to make his office). During the past five years, the liberals have sometimes been at odds with Chris Patten, but they have also prospered under an administration committed to expanding democracy. Soon Patten will be replaced with a chief executive who prefers to talk more about livelihood issues and Chinese values than democracy. Some tensions are evident between Martin Lee and Tung, who clearly disapproves of Lee's speeches abroad and articles in Western news media. When Lee told European parliamentarians that Hong Kong's freedoms and rule of law were at risk, Tung very publicly issued a challenge, accused him of writing articles painting an unfavorable portrait of the region's prospects after turnover and generally "bad-mouthing" Hong Kong.

How to deal with China and its handover committees has split the democrats in several ways. Frederick Fung, for example, joined the Preparatory Committee. His party also agreed to serve on the temporary body and won four seats (same as it has in Legco). Soon after, ten party members staged a high-profile walkout. The Democratic Party declined to join the provisional legislature but has had some difficulties in its own ranks too. A formerly obscure Democratic Party urban councillor, Dominic Chan, was expelled after he broke ranks and applied for a seat on the provisional legislature. He was rewarded for his defection with a seat. Chan calls himself a realistic Democrat in wanting to cooperate more closely on the handover and claims that many other party members sympathize with his position. If so, they've kept their thoughts to themselves. No more "defections" have surfaced. Even independent Christine Loh, who has followed her own path, found her new web site sabotaged. On top of her picture were superimposed the words, *lies, lies, lies!* The web site designer, a disgruntled former Loh supporter who lives in Australia, admitted doing it because Loh says that she favors open dialogue with Beijing.

Some of the more radical democrats seem to be giving up on electoral politics. Emily Lau says she's not sure if she will run again. Indeed, she has been sounding rather depressed of late. "I'll need a job," she told students during a recent symposium in Charlotte, North Carolina, adding that she might have a hard time finding one because of her uncompromising views. But she is married to a barrister, so some of her poor-mouthing may be a little bit for effect. As a prelude to what might come, Lau and some like-minded legislators, who are grouped loosely under the name "Frontier", staged a noisy protest outside the Convention Centre when Tung was selected chief and were briefly detained by police for lying down on the road. The more mainstream democrats prefer to use the courts. Martin Lee says his party will challenge any laws passed by the provisional legislature in the courts before the handover date. He has no other option, he says, since Tung has apparently decided that some bills must be ready for his signature on July 1. Just before he left for his North American trip, Lee and some other members had a meeting with Tung. I attended the press conference that followed. Nobody had changed his position. Lee said that the chief had admonished them to "think thrice" about taking the provisional legislature to court, and he made a lawyerly joke about going to court if they try to pass the third reading.

Their credibility abroad and access to decision makers and the major Western news media gives the democrats a major asset. Which may be why so many prominent liberals have spent so much time outside of the territory these days. Lee had hardly returned from an important swing through Europe than he was off on a thirteen-city tour of Canada and the US. The trip will culminate in Washington, where he is to receive the 1997 Democracy Award from the National Endowment for Democracy (an organization created to do openly the work of influencing politics in other countries that the CIA had done surreptitiously). Emily Lau was also in the US, where she was received by members of the National

Security Council in the White House, (she reportedly advised the NSC staff to be more active in challenging Beijing and suggested that one way to do it would be to postpone the planned visits to China by Vice President Al Gore (who went to China anyway). She also was cordially greeted by very conservative and, as the chairman of the Senate Foreign Relations Committee, powerful Senator Jesse Helms. He refused to meet Allen Lee during his trip to the US because he serves on the Provisional Legislature.

While in Canada and America, she also spoke with newspaper columnists, including Mary McGrory of the *Washington Post* and radio talk show hosts Jim Hightower and Bay Buchanan, and, in fact, anyone else who would listen, including college students in Charlotte. At the North Carolina school she met two Hong Kong students, who had recently enrolled. One of them asked Lau if she didn't sometimes feel that whatever will be will be and that trying to change things was futile. Visibly irritated, Lau took the challenge: "That's the problem with Hong Kong people. How can you expect other people to support you if you are not willing to fight for yourself?"

\*     \*     \*     \*

Its siren sounding a throaty farewell, its blue ensign flying proudly from the mast, the luxury liner *Queen Elizabeth 2* slowly pulled away from Ocean Terminal after making its last port call here under British rule. From the fantail, a contingent of retiring British civil servants and their families bound for Blighty at Hong Kong taxpayers' expense watched the famous skyline recede. The day before, another larger group had boarded the *Oriana* of the P&O Line for the leisurely cruise home. Former Director of Social Welfare Ian Strachan wasn't about to miss this once-in-a-lifetime opportunity. He flew *back* to Hong Kong from Britain just so he could catch the boat ride home. "It's like leaving an old friend," said Strachan of the colony he came out to serve 32 years earlier.

He and his shipmates were enjoying one of the last colonial perks: "standard homeward passage by sea". That magical phrase used to be in every British and Commonwealth government officials' contract until it was finally dropped as obsolete in 1984. The Victorians could hardly have foreseen a day when "standard passage" meant travel by air and that steamships would become floating pleasure palaces, complete with casinos, swimming pools and day-trips to exotic ports of call. In 1992 the government tried to remove the perk from everyone's contract, not just new hires. That naturally provoked an outrage in the civil service, the expatriate side of it anyway. The government backed down in the face of possible breach of contract lawsuits. Still, 697 British and other expatriate civil servants qualify for the luxury cruise home at an average cost of US$7,400 per person—more than double a first-class airline ticket.

While the newspapers sometimes make an issue of this extravagance and sometimes questions are raised in Legco, its doubtful that many Hongkongers are put out. The place is simply too rich for anyone to worry about such trifling expenses. After all, this is a city where the budget surplus, announced a week after the ships departed, is US$4 *billion,* nine times as great as the original projection. Probably it is sufficient to send one more public servant home in style. Though he arrived after 1984, Patten will also enjoy "standard homeward passage by sea"—on the Royal Yacht *Britannia*—on the evening of July 1. In fact, he may be at sea only long enough to reach a non-Chinese airport to fly to his vacation home in France, where he'll probably spend his first months unwinding and writing about his Asian experiences.

While the British civil servants were enjoying their *Love Boat* cruise home, the Financial Secretary was droning his way through the 1997/98 budget address. Strangely, he is not getting much applause for managing the surplus or for piling up the almost obscene financial reserves that the colony has—US$46 billion alone, or more than US$100 billion if the fund kept to support the Hong Kong dollar is included. Outside the Legco building police dismantled a bomb, which carried some ominous slogans. These accused the government of "ignoring the rapid rise of property prices and the masses having to live in poverty". The "bomb" was in fact a fake filled with sand, but its presence was sobering in a colony that in recent years has been so free of terrorism that the police hardly bother to check people or their bags when they go into the public gallery. And it shows that beneath the general contentment lurk a few dangers.

The *Post* was downright bolshevik in its scathing commentary of the new budget under the headline: HONG KONG'S SHAME.

"What is needed is an economic strategy which will help share our wealth so that everyone can enjoy the fruits of their labor, regardless of their job." The Hong Kong "masses" are, in fact, doing pretty well, but undeniably a significant minority is falling behind and receives niggardly assistance, despite efforts under Patten to boost social welfare spending.

In the curious world of Hong Kong–China politics, the communists in China are the misers on public spending. In 1995, China's representative in Hong Kong complained of modest rises in social spending under Patten's administration, claiming that they were like an "out-of-control car heading for a crash". The financial secretary was forced to defend the budget from those who called it a kowtow to Beijing. Since the spending plan straddles the handover date, it had to be negotiated between China and Britain. In theory, Hong Kong will have more say in its budget in subsequent years. It may be that the Chinese are really fearful of boosting the social safety net in Hong Kong at a time when it is systematically dismantling the one on the mainland. In any case, China's fears seem excessive. The British will leave behind combined reserves—what Patten has called the "biggest dowry since Cleopatra"—more than China's own foreign currency reserves.

The Democrats met for the second time with Tung and urged him to take steps to curb property price rises and boost social spending by a modest US$35 a month. I suspect that he is much more receptive to these livelihood issues than he is to the party's complaints about the provisional legislature. I may be wrong, but I got the impression that Tung had a consciousness-awakening experience during his own campaign, somewhat like the one that has often been attributed to John F. Kennedy when he campaigned among the poor in West Virginia. Tung seemed visibly moved touring public housing estates and visiting the cage people. In any case, in his remarks in public he has put much more emphasis on these matters while downplaying constitutional development and advancing democracy, the hallmarks of the Patten administration. He recently announced that he plans to set up three task forces to help formulate new policies for affordable housing, improving education, and better care for the elderly. Meanwhile, the well-off have some reasons to toast Donald Tsang. At lunch at the Jockey Club I noticed a poster announcing lower prices for French vintages. Thanks to the new budget, the duty on imported wine has been cut by 30 percent.

# March 1997

*"Hong Kong is like a Rolls-Royce. All you have to do is slip into the driving seat, switch on the ignition and away you go."*

As THE DAY FADED into late afternoon, the Fijians vigorously performed their traditional *cibi* war dance to psych out their opponents. The force seems to have been with them. The Fijians beat the South Africans to win the 21st playing of the Hong Kong Rugby Sevens. The Sevens is a scaled-down version of the traditional 15-man game. It more or less got its start in Hong Kong when the first tournament was held in 1976. Superficially, it resembles American football. The players carry the pigskin across the goal line for the score (strangely called a "try", even though it seems more like a success to me).

Yet in many ways it's more like basketball, a fast moving, high scoring game with a lot of elegant passing and fancy footwork. It's not unusual for a team to rack up 50 points or more in a 20-minute game or to make the first score within seconds of the opening kickoff. It was almost impossible to get tickets for the Sevens this year. Of course, Hong Kong was hosting the World Cup championships. More to the point, many people felt, despite numerous assurances to the contrary, that the games might not survive the coming of Chinese sovereignty, now exactly 100 days away.

For the Sevens is more than just a sports contest. It is the Hong Kong expat social event of the year, a kind of spring rite of passage. Much of the color and a little of the action takes place in the stands, where the otherwise starchy stockbrokers and currency dealers let their hair down and their inhibitions loose (though their behavior is much less loutish—and certainly less violent—than soccer hooligans in Britain). The fact that a couple dozen national teams compete and the games are short presents an ever-changing panorama of nationalism in which to draw out loyalties of Hong Kong's motley international set. Over the years, the Sevens has spawned its own tribal rituals, traditions, even celebrities. Pictures of Martin Hollis, also known as the "Pieman", his huge, naked belly fully displayed standing in his prominent spot in the bleachers, are always published in the English-language newspapers. For some reason, it is obligatory to boo the Australian team when it goes on the field. The stands are full of people with the British Union Jack painted on their faces or wearing hats that look like kiwis. And, of course, no Sevens tournament is complete without at least one streaker.

I don't know what the Chinese majority makes of all this. Perhaps nothing much. It can't have much interest in the Hong Kong team, even if it did win a division this year. Apparently only one certifiable Chinese player graced the roster. Two high-profile commercial sponsors, the Hongkong and Shanghai Banking Corporation and Cathay Pacific, both pillars of the British establishment for generations, announced earlier this year that they plan to end their generous annual support with this year's games. That probably will not seriously impact the finances of the game, which are well established, but it was symbolic. The two companies talked a lot about "reordering" their advertising priorities and so on, but they probably don't feel it expedient to be formally associated with such an overwhelmingly expatriate event. For them it is sort of like taking down pictures of opium dealers from their office walls.

Still, it is probably too early to predict the demise of the Sevens. The games are a big money-spinner, and every segment of society here certainly respects that. Tung Chee-hwa made a brief appearance on Saturday, which seemed to give the tournament the imprimatur of the new regime. He spent most of the weekend, however, presiding over several local events marking 100 days until the handover. In one, 3,000 children ran, between them, the equivalent of the 2,000 or so kilometers from Hong Kong to Beijing. It was one of several hokey events being staged these days to build up Chinese enthusiasm for the coming transfer. I wonder if he will he be in the stands this time next year handing out the silverware to the winning players? It is significant that China joined the International Rugby Union this year, and a team from the People's Liberation Army played and beat a team from Britain's Black Watch regiment in a game of "tens", another rugby variant a few days before. True, rugby does not have deep roots locally. But that doesn't mean the end of the Sevens, so long as a significant expatriate population still lives here. I don't imagine that the Chinese would begrudge us a blowout at least once a year.

Chris Patten sounded pretty satisfied with himself on the radio in the *Letter to Hong Kong* marking 100 days to the transition. He referred to a recent poll that showed 90 percent of the people were happy with their lives in Hong Kong, 73 percent with the government. "The way we run things here is very effective, which is why I'm delighted that our first-class team of senior officials will all be traveling through the transition together, and I hope they'll be in office for many years to come," he said. "Hong Kong is, as I said recently, a smoothly functioning community. It's like a Rolls-Royce. All you need to do if you're in charge is to slip into the driving seat, switch on the ignition and away you go. I don't quite see the point in lifting the hood to tinker with the engine. That only raises worries about whether it will work so well, and whether you may be persuaded by some people to start stripping it down for spare parts . . . I happen to think myself that Hong Kong needs governing with a light touch. That you can't turn the clock back on what Hong Kong has become, any more than you can reverse the countdown. I hope that China's advisers will stop seeing Hong Kong in terms of a struggle, will stop tilting against so-called British windmills." Patten's personal ratings have been going up of late, not surprising considering he isn't really doing much these days. It is Tung who is getting chewed up in public opinion polls over such contentious matters as the provisional legislature and plans to reinstate some of the older language of the Public Order and Societies Ordinances, all of which Patten opposes.

China's official *People's Daily* marked the 100-day benchmark in its own inimitable fashion. It issued a long screed detailing what it termed a sad story of "violence, blood, humiliation and struggle", meaning 156 years of British colonial rule in Hong Kong. The Chinese have been picking at that particular scab a lot in the past few months. Across the border in Shenzhen, and in Shanghai, Chinese movie director Xie Jin is doing the final editing of his cast-of-thousands spectacular called *The Opium War,* reportedly the costliest movie in Chinese film history. It is supposed to open on June 30 in Beijing and probably the following day in Hong Kong. As the film's promotional brochure says, it is "dedicated to the great moment in history—the return of Hong Kong to China on July 1997". It doesn't sound like one will hear very much positive about Britain's legacy such as its splendid civil service or the rule of law or indeed anything that conflicts with the official Chinese line about the handover: it is righting an ancient wrong; 1997 ushers in an unspecified but incomparably better tomorrow.

In Hong Kong, Britons are getting another rude reminder that their one mark of privileged status is ending. All over town large posters proclaim in red and blue letters: BRITISH CITIZENS: CHANGES IN IMMIGRATION CONTROLS. They remind everyone that, as of April 1, British people must register for visas and working permits like any other expats, unless they are already permanent residents. In many other ways the trappings of British rule are disappearing rapidly. The royal coat-of-arms in the marriage halls is coming down or being covered over with a red curtain—although strangely, there seems to be a rush to wed on the last day of business before the change of sovereignty. It must be either because couples want to have the royal seal on their marriage certificates or because June 29 is a particularly propitious date. Pick up a newspaper: a front page picture shows the White Ensign being lowered at Stonecutters Island, the last location of HMS *Tamar,* once a real ship that first docked in Hong Kong on April 11, 1897, exactly 100 years ago, becoming the floating headquarters of the British forces. Later it became the name of the naval basin. Ironically, the British commander will end his last few days in Hong Kong on another floating headquarters, the Royal Navy frigate HMS *Chatham.*

Postage stamps bearing the profile of Queen Elizabeth II have become collectors items. They are the last in a long line of definitives (regular issues) that stretches back to the first Hong Kong stamp, issued in 1862, featuring the head of Queen Victoria. The "queen's head" stamps were discontinued in January in favor of a transitional version depicting the colony's cityscape. Other commemorative stamps bearing the royal cartouche in the corner (EIIR and crown) will be issued through June 30. When in March the post office cleared its remaining stocks, people wanting to buy them by the sheet stretched for a kilometer. Many apparently were from the mainland, where sheets of stamps are traded like so many gilt-edged securities. Even in Hong Kong a complete set of the last regular issue, which has a nominal face value of about HK$114, has been trading on the secondary market for HK$1,000 or more. Many dealers shake their heads in wonderment. After all, there is no scarcity. On the last day of sale, more than 250,000 sheets, about 20 million stamps, were sold. That doesn't count the millions sold since they were first issued in 1992. Indeed, the government has started printing a disclaimer, similar to the one for mutual funds, on advertisements announcing new issues: "The market value of stamps can go down as well as up."

The post office is having a hard time explaining that it is not profiteering from all the handover hoopla. Perhaps not—the stamps are sold at face value—but certainly making a bundle. It reportedly took in more than *US$100 million* from philatelic sales in the past year. As its latest marketing ploy, the postal service plans to reissue a set of stamps it first put up for sale in 1991 to celebrate its 150th anniversary. They will be valid for that one day only, after which letters bearing them will be returned to sender. The stamps feature pictures of the red Royal Mail post boxes with portraits of the five monarchs (not counting Edward VIII) since Hong Kong's founding. But if you want the real thing, the post office has been auctioning off the cast-iron boxes, a few of them dating from the reign of George v. As for the others, they're busy unscrewing the EIIRs, replacing them with a P for post and painting them the new Hongkong Post green.

Is it wise to be taking down all of this colonial regalia? Already some travel agents are grumbling that bookings have fallen off after the handover date. Some of them blame this on the bad press they think Hong Kong has been getting. But could being a British crown colony in Asia also have a special appeal? In this respect Macau, which by coincidence just marked 1,000 days until its return to China, may have had a shrewder outlook. For the past five years it has been working overtime to preserve and refurbish the architectural heritage of 450 years of Portuguese rule. Everywhere is evidence of major restoration work in explosions of reds, oranges, yellows and pinks. When I first visited Macau in 1987, the plaza of the Leal Senado, the very heart of the old town, was seedy and rundown. Now all of the buildings that front the town square have been lovingly restored. Portuguese craftsmen installed a Mediterranean-style mosaic of wavy black and white on the pavement.

This preservation program has political undertones, since the administration is intent on preserving evidence of the European presence long after 1999. That is one crucial difference between Macau and its much larger neighbor. Hong Kong worries incessantly about its precious local autonomy, which it defines almost entirely in terms of the rule of law and democracy. Macau, a much smaller place, could easily be absorbed into a greater Zhuhai, the faceless, characterless Chinese special economic zone just outside the colorful old border gates. I asked Luis Durão, chief of the government's department of cultural preservation about this. "What we want to do is to preserve the uniqueness of Macau, the Mediterranean culture brought by Portugal to China. It created a mix that is unique to this area, maybe to the world."

Well, Hong Kong doesn't have many colonial-era buildings left, but at least it will keep the double-decker buses.

\*　\*　\*　\*

The mother had resisted repeated calls to surrender. She even threatened to kill herself rather than break up her family, so the authorities were not taking any chances. Twenty immigration officers, with a dozen firemen standing by in reserve, were deployed to apprehend Chung Chau Chuk-ngan and her eight-year-old daughter and whisk them across the border to China. The whole drama, of course, took place in full view of a pack of Hong Kong journalists, who photographed the screaming child being hauled away by two grim-faced immigration officers. The family's two smaller children, born in Hong Kong and thus legal, were left in the care of social workers. Ugly scenes such as this have become common in Hong Kong in the final days leading to the handover. The colony is coping with a tide of children entering illegally because their parents believe, despite vigorous denials, that they can remain here after July 1.

The problem arises because the Basic Law guarantees that children born from parents who are Hong Kong residents have the right to live here. An important catch: they have to enter legally to claim that right. "If they sneak into the territory before their status can be confirmed, they will be sent back," promised Tung during a television interview. When the Basic Law was drafted in the late 1980s, nobody fully realized all of the consequences stemming from the economic and social integration of Hong Kong and its hinterland. These days about 80 percent of Hong Kong's manufacturing base has relocated across the border to take advantage of lower production costs. Every day tens of thousands of people, most of them men, cross into China to work as factory managers, truck drivers and businessmen. Some people have taken advantage of the lower property costs to buy retirement homes there. The inevitable happens. They meet and marry Chinese women, have children and, naturally enough, they want to bring their families back to join them in Hong Kong. "You can't blame China for this problem; it's entirely Hong Kong's fault. We've been too romantic," said legislator David Chu.

But in trying to bring their children home, they encounter many difficulties. By mutual agreement, the Chinese issue only 150 "one-way permits", a day—about 50,000 a year—allowing mainlanders to enter Hong Kong to stay permanently. About a third of them are reserved for children. The result is an artificial scarcity and the inevitable consequence—corruption. Families in China without connections or unwilling to pay exorbitant bribes may have to wait years to get the permits. Many naturally lose patience and are willing to risk their lives and savings hiring the aptly named "snakeheads", illegal immigrant smugglers, to sneak them or their children into Hong Kong hidden away on junks like so many crates of illegal cigarettes. Recently the marine police on smuggler patrol broke off shadowing a suspicious vessel when the smugglers apparently threw a body over the side. It turned out to be a decoy, just a bundle of straw, but the notion that the snakeheads might actually jettison their human cargoes to escape capture was sobering.

Many illegal immigrants end up on the thirteenth floor of the immigration headquarters in the so-called surrender center, a small waiting room lined with hard wooden benches. They wait there to plead their case to an immigration officer. It is a sad place, a place where families, briefly reunited, are broken up, where pregnant women are separated from their husbands, where people find that the life savings they invested in illegal entry into the colony have evaporated just as surely as if they had placed them on a roulette table in Macau. Cheng Xianglan, fourteen, sneaked into Hong Kong, she says, to take care of a mentally ill father and her younger brother, who, born here, has a legal right to stay. Chen Guangming, twelve, has a father with a worsening heart condition. She's afraid that if she is deported, she might not be able to see him again. Not a few of those seeking hardship exemptions have elderly fathers or husbands in failing health. They had sought wives in poorer Chinese villages, perhaps, because they weren't considered very good marriage material by local women.

But despite the hard luck stories, despite the ugly images of mothers and children being led away in handcuffs, the government is reluctant to take any action that would even hint at a relaxation of border rules. "It would open the floodgates," Chu told me later. Officially about 40,000 children living in China are believed to have the right to live in Hong Kong. That doesn't sound too bad against a population of more than six million. But Guangdong Province authorities raised the anxiety level higher when they claimed that the true number was more like 130,000, and unofficial estimates range up to 400,000. If those higher figures are true, they would be equal to the number of children in Hong Kong attending primary classes now, putting enormous strains on schools and housing, already becoming a sore point with many residents. "The rate of entry is growing faster than the solutions," says Chu.

The last time that Hong Kong faced the prospect of such a large and sudden influx of migrants was in the aftermath of the Chinese civil war in the early 1950s. Thousands of defeated Nationalist soldiers and refugees from the communists entered the territory. For years they lived in squatter camps until, in the 1970s, Hong Kong undertook a massive program of public housing. In recent years, the Chinese have cooperated in controlling migration. Indeed, whenever Beijing was displeased with something about Hong Kong, one of its favorite tactics was simply to threaten not to take any illegal immigrants back. That usually brought Hong Kong to heel fast. These days the Chinese army and paramilitary forces routinely practice repel-boarders drills to turn back any of its citizens who might be under the illusion that just because Hong Kong is becoming a part of China, anyone who wants to can move there. China has a floating population, now estimated as high as 90 million, made up of the unemployed from the country, gravitating to the cities to try to find work. It would not be surprising if they gravitated to what will become incomparably China's richest city.

\*   \*   \*   \*

In an elegant ballroom at the Marriott Hotel, Anthony Lin, Christie's suave, Mandarin-speaking director, brought the hammer down on the last auction before the handover—or as one of the directors preferred to say, the *first* auction before the handover. Over at the Furama Hotel, arch rival Sotheby's was also holding its last pre-1997 sale. Among the many beautiful things going under the gavel were a few that might well be illegal to sell if the auctions were being held in, say, Shanghai instead of Hong Kong. Like many other aspects of life, capitalist Hong Kong and the communist mainland approach the antiques trade from diametrically opposite directions. Beijing forbids the sale and export of relics older than 200 years without a license. Free-trading Hong Kong has no export controls beyond a few restrictions on gold movements and sale of opium implements. Zhang Wenbin of the Chinese State Bureau of Preservation of Cultural Relics said flatly: "Chinese laws on the protection of cultural relics will not be applied in Hong Kong."

The Hong Kong Special Administrative Region will be a separate customs territory free to promulgate its own policy on relics, if it chooses to do so. At the moment, the new administration has much more pressing matters on its plate than controlling the antiques trade. For that matter, Tung is himself a collector of old Chinese artifacts. Even so, as in other aspects of the transition, skeptics in Hong Kong are unwilling to risk their businesses or precious collections on promises. Half of the exhibits at Singapore's recently opened Asian Civilizations Museum, for example, are on loan from well-known Hong Kong collectors. And it isn't just neighborliness at work. For collectors of rare antiques, holding a foreign exhibition is like obtaining a foreign passport; it is a hedge against the uncertainties of life in Hong Kong after the handover.

The major auction houses, Christie's and Sotheby's, profess to be unconcerned about the handover. "Nothing under existing law prevents us from selling, say, 15th-century porcelain, and we see no future law preventing us either," Colin Sheaf, a Christie's director, told me. The two big auctioneers, which just wound up record spring sales in the territory, can afford to be sanguine about the future. Antiques make up a relatively small segment of their trade and not necessarily the most lucrative one either. Most of their sales are of very expensive jade jewelry, contemporary Chinese paintings, rare postage stamps and property in Britain. This year Sotheby's even sold composer Andrew Lloyd Webber's wine cellar to a collector in Hong Kong. Both auction houses could still make a lot of money selling nothing older than one hundred years.

But ancient Chinese ceramics remain the backbone of the antiques trade among local dealers. That becomes quickly obvious strolling down Hollywood Road to "Cat Street" (officially Upper Lascar Row), the traditional focus of the antiques trade, where the windows are packed with neolithic bowls, Han dynasty judges, Tang dynasty horses. "I'm astounded at the amount of early Chinese artifacts now in Hong Kong," says veteran dealer Lucille Vessa, who has been watching the antiques trade for 26 years from her perch at Honeychurch Antiques.

I doubt that the authorities in China are overly exercised about the trade in tomb artifacts, which has grown rapidly as a result of the country's modernization. Graves are dug up for foundations, and peasants are happy to sell ancient chests or wooden beds for more modern appliances. Indeed, the genuinely old ceramic horses, camels and statues that fill Hong Kong shops were themselves mass produced in "factories" and have little archaeological or artistic merit. Chinese collectors tend to disdain funerary objects, though they are popular with Westerners.

"Most of the things you find in antique shops are not cultural relics," says Karin Weber, a dealer, who specializes in Chinese furniture. "The really valuable things are mostly in museums or in private collections."

She and other traders take a cautiously optimistic view that their businesses will survive the handover. But many dealers are still nervous about the future. Some shops in the neighborhood look like they have been abandoned, boarded up with FOR RENT signs in the front. "One or two big dealers have sold out and moved away because they got worried." It may be a long time before they feel confident enough to come back. In the meantime, art museums from Singapore to Denver are expanding their Chinese departments thanks to the insecurities of Hong Kong collectors.

# April 1997                                    -70 DRYS

*"Five Chinese generals cost much less than one British general."*

A DEMONSTRATION IN FAVOR OF DEMONSTRATIONS—a political rally called to object to plans to add restrictions on public protests and foreign funding of political parties—took place in Victoria Park on Sunday. I saw the usual red, yellow and black banners: SAY NO TO FAKE CONSULTATIONS and WE HAVE THE RIGHT TO HAVE LINKS WITH FOREIGN ASSOCIATIONS, among them. Liberal legislators and trade unionists gave fiery speeches. Young people tied themselves together with a large rope and wore gags, symbolizing the loss of free speech that they believe will occur if these amendments are put into effect. Then about 500 people shuffled off toward Hennessy Road and wound their way through Wan Chai to Chater Garden in Central, where they listened to more speeches and then dispersed. Another Sunday in the park in Hong Kong.

Hardly a weekend—sometimes hardly a day—passes without some group or other exercising their freedom to protest. When dissident Wang Dan was arrested, tried and imprisoned last year with China's usual efficiency, protesters literally camped out for days at the entrance to Xinhua's Happy Valley headquarters. A hundred or more demonstrations occurred outside Xinhua alone in 1996. The Alliance in Support of the Patriotic Democratic Movement in China is gearing up for an enormous rally in Victoria Park. It will be the last memorial for those who lost their lives in the bloody June 4, 1989 crackdown in Beijing before the handover. But some of the protesters concentrated on more personal concerns. One day the elderly may lobby legislators for old-age pensions, or pig farmers complain about new laws preventing them from dumping waste in the water. Last week, people from my neighborhood rallied in downtown Central to protest plans by a local property developer to sell off apartment parking spaces at exorbitant prices.

Among politically active Hongkongers, passions have been running high since the Tung administration released its consultation paper outlining reasons for certain restrictions on public demonstrations and the banning of foreign contributions to local political parties. (The document, "Civil Liberties and Social Order", was released on April 9, the same day that Martin Lee was receiving a Democracy Award in Washington. Poor timing.) Some Democratic Party members denounced the whole consultation procedure as a sham at a forum held in the Hong Kong Space Museum to brief local municipal and district board officers. Some pushing and shoving with some of the pro-Beijing people took place outside the venue. "We're here to listen to different views," Tung's policy coordinator, Michael Suen, said plaintively.

Chris Patten, slipping comfortably into his new role as a kind of opposition leader, made his views clear on the radio program, *Letter to Hong Kong:* "In the last few weeks, we've witnessed a vigorous debate about civil liberties in Hong Kong. Chinese officials decided that Hong Kong has too much freedom and that it needs to be curtailed. Not because the laws which protect our freedoms infringe the Basic Law. They don't. Not because they have undermined our stability. They haven't—even some of those who advocate the changes seem to be admitting at the same time that Hong Kong is a very stable, moderate place. Nor can it be said that exercising our civil liberties as we do has made us less prosperous. That proposition is absurd. No, the decision seems to be based on their wish to have a tighter control over life here. They don't—they should, but they don't—trust Hong Kong. . . . With so much good happening here, with so much good to show ourselves, why embroil Hong Kong in these unnecessary arguments which so worry our friends and partners overseas, as well as worrying us?"

Why, indeed? The Tung administration insists that the legislation must be adopted to avoid a "legal vacuum" on July 1, although it isn't obvious why the social order would collapse if such changes were not on the books immediately after the handover. Even such a staunch pro-China supporter as David Chu questions the wisdom of the rush-job. "Are they needed to control demonstrations on the handover day? No. Passing the legislation will only increase the likelihood of such demonstrations."

Tung, nevertheless, pushes doggedly ahead. Some fine-tuning may yet occur, but the amendments almost certainly will be adopted substantially the way they were proposed. I think he recognizes that this is China's bottom line; he might as well get it behind him now. Most people in Hong Kong are shrewd enough to recognize why Tung is acting now, though the brouhaha is costing him some of his popularity in public opinion polls. The main criticism is less the amendments themselves as what appears to be undue enthusiasm about carrying Beijing's water.

Everyone seems to agree that the consultation paper was put together sloppily by Tung's skeleton transition staff. He doesn't yet have the services of the government's skilled law drafting department. It is official policy not to cooperate in such in matters. One example of the general looseness: proposed changes in the Societies Ordinance say that "aliens" cannot make campaign contributions to local political parties. This is absurd since long-time resident aliens, like me, can vote in local elections and even serve in the Legislative Council. The repeated references to the need to protect "national security" drew much comment. They were not in the old ordinances (probably because the British never worried that anything that happened in a small colony half-way around the world could in any way impinge on their own national security). As Elsie Leung, the secretary of justice-designate, said pithily in her otherwise rather lawyerly defense of including this loaded term in the document, "Hong Kong is a stone's throw from China."

Is it a coincidence that China itself is rewriting some laws in this same area? In March, the National People's Congress adopted a new criminal code replacing "counter-revolutionary" offenses—a word redolent of old-style class struggle—with a new category of crimes against national security. Another element of Tung's amendments is a ban on foreign support or funding for those considered subversive. Ironically, the new Labour government in Britain says it too plans to tighten the existing laws against foreign campaign contributions. They have a special grievance: much money has poured into the Conservative Party's financial coffers in recent years from, if not exactly "foreign sources", at least from outside of the United Kingdom, namely from Hong Kong business tycoons. On the list for a sizable £50,000 is one C.H. Tung.

Any changes will have to be approved by the provisional legislature. It finally got down to business when it debated a bill setting forth a schedule of public holidays for the new SAR. Presumably, this is one of the "essential" pieces of legislation to be taken care of by the provisional body even before July 1. Another "essential" bill, making it illegal to desecrate the SAR and Chinese national flags, will also be tabled. The significance of the rather innocuous holiday legislation? It is likely to be the first bill passed before the handover date, and thus might become the vehicle on which to challenge the legality of the provisional legislature and its laws.

\*    \*    \*    \*

Even as Tung was taking a pounding in Hong Kong, Martin Lee was being feted in Washington. The President of the United States does not usually have the time to meet visiting members of small, foreign provincial legislatures. And no doubt President Bill Clinton would have preferred to duck meeting Lee, which could only have served to antagonize Beijing at a time when he is trying to improve relations. But Lee has already become a darling of Congress, not to mention a shining beacon of democracy in Asia. So the president had a lot of pressure to find time for him. Wrote the *Washington Post:* "President Clinton's meeting with Hong Kong's leading democrat, Martin Lee, should open an unabashed American campaign to defend Hong Kong's endangered liberties." In the end, Clinton "dropped in" on a meeting officially scheduled with

Vice President Al Gore, the same tactic he would later use to meet with the Dalai Lama, and for much the same reason.

Tung called off his own planned trip to the US, claiming that he "had too much work to do." It may have been a wise decision, though clumsily executed. He could have waited for a few weeks until after Lee's diplomatic coup had faded. Then he still could have found some diplomatic excuse, like being called to Beijing. Of course, when Lee engineered his meeting with Clinton, he had upped the political stakes considerably. Tung could not risk a snub. Even if Clinton were willing to meet with him, some domestic crisis could intervene to force a cancellation. That would have been a loss of face too awful to contemplate. Further, the American press would have chewed him up over the changes to the civil liberties ordinances and the provisional legislature. It is probably prudent that Tung delayed his trip until some time after July Then, he may have a good story to tell. If he doesn't, spin control will be of little help.

Strangely, Lee doesn't seem to be getting the hosannas in Hong Kong that he might have expected after his triumph in the US and Canada (where he met with Prime Minister Jean Chretien). Even *Apple Daily* was critical. Minky Worden, Martin Lee's legislative assistant, complained that Hong Kong's newspapers generally negative reaction was further evidence that local newspapers were adjusting their coverage of issues to please China. Not surprisingly, David Chu was critical, when we chewed over events at his new office-cum-wine-cellar-cum-private-kitchen. (For a man who serves on two legislatures and runs a property company, Chu seems to have a lot of time on his hands these days.) After discussing his latest hobby, aerobatic flying, the talk turned to Lee's trip.

"This has serious, long-term consequences. It's not kid's play. Relations between China and the US are finely balanced at the moment. We basically violated the most important principle that allows for our existence, meaning 'one country, two systems'. [Premier] Li Peng must be thinking, 'that little twit is affecting our relations with the most powerful nation on earth'."

Strong words, but no doubt Hong Kong is emerging as a potential sore point in America's often delicate relations with China. It is a touchstone for many critics in Congress, where China seems to have replaced the Soviet Union as the new Evil Empire. Quite a number of US legislators, including Speaker of the House Newt Gingrich, passed through the colony during the Easter recess. They came away with two fixed ideas about Hong Kong: Tung is basically China's stooge and on Beijing's orders he is systematically dismantling Hong Kong's liberties. On his return, Gingrich even floated the idea of renewing China's "most-favored nation" trading status (only a handful of nations do not have it) for only six months. Apparently, Chris Patten later managed to dissuade him. Added to this is the smoldering scandal over allegedly illegal campaign contributions to the US Democratic Party, which has exploded into strange and ominous new directions. China was dragged into "Donorgate"—now evidently in its "Chinagate" phase—on the wings of media reports suggesting that the Chinese government had tried to steer campaign contributions to at least six members of Congress. Beijing's embassy in Washington categorically denied the allegations.

No one has provided firm evidence that China's government tried to influence American politicians illegally. Indeed, some of the details are a little suspect. One of the six lawmakers to whom the Chinese purportedly considered giving money was Representative Nancy Pelosi (Democrat, California), one of China's fiercest critics and a vocal opponent of its most-favored nation trading status. Even optimists in Beijing are unlikely to turn her around. It was painful to watch Vice President Gore go through contortions to avoid looking like he was toasting China's Premier Li Peng, the "butcher of Tiananmen", during his visit to Beijing.

For several years, Americans have comprised the largest and most influential foreign community in Hong Kong. By various counts, more than 40,000 of us live here; and the numbers are rising nearly ten percent a year. The numbers of Britons has declined to an estimated 20,000. Many Americans are influential in Hong Kong affairs. Henry Townsend, for example, heads the local airport authority, currently building a massive new airport on an artificial island. Minky Worden, who used to write speeches for former Attorney General Richard Thornburgh, now crafts them for Martin Lee. Paul Cheng runs Inchcape, one of Hong Kong's oldest trading companies, and also serves in Legco (as do two other American citizens). Ira Kaye, a local businessman, holds an OBE (Order of the British Empire) for his charity work. Victor Fung, a former professor at Harvard Business School, chairs the Hong Kong Trade Development Council. Many local residents have close connections with the US because they were educated there; about 14,000 are now in American classrooms. Or they have relatives who moved there. Tung, himself, lived for many years in the US and, until his recent election, was a long-time member of the American Chamber of Commerce in Hong Kong.

Add to that US$14 billion in direct investments (not counting personal real estate, and small businesses) plus about US$50 billion in loans. It is clear that Americans have a considerable stake in Hong Kong's future. The United States will, then, increasingly take on the role of protector of Hong Kong's freedoms and autonomy. This was probably inevitable in that Washington has more influence in Beijing than London does. Washington's official interest in Hong Kong is spelled out in the US–Hong Kong Policy Act of 1992. It requires periodic reports to Congress that China is living up to the agreement it made with Britain to allow post-1997 Hong Kong a "high degree of autonomy". The legislation has practical implications: many aspects of America's relations with the future SAR, from extraditing accused criminals to observing various commercial treaties, presume that Hong Kong will continue to be a distinct legal entity, separate and apart from China. But some of China's recent actions—such as disbanding the elected legislature and invalidating some civil rights laws—have convinced many congressmen that another law is needed. Hence, the Hong Kong Reversion Act, which recently passed the House of Representatives 416-1 and awaits Senate action. It declares that the US will take an official interest in the degree to which China respects the rule of law, freedom of the press and the unrestricted flow of information.

Despite these official misgivings, much progress is actually being made in regularizing relations with a post-1997 Hong Kong. Agreements have been reached to keep the rather large US consulate in place, though the military spies in the Defense Liaison Office will have to wear civvies on the job. Washington recently announced that it would recognize the SAR passport. Happy to get some good news from this quarter for a change, Tung quickly issued a press release: "We invite US citizens to continue enjoying Hong Kong's attractions as a major international business, financial and tourism center." Treaties have been negotiated to extradite criminals and exchange prisoners, although they still await Senate action. Hong Kong, absent the sight of American naval vessels anchored in the harbor and sailors in the streets, would not seem like Hong Kong. So Americans found it welcome news that Beijing has also been rather generous in allowing continued port calls by the fleet. Since about 60 to 80 ships call each year, Hongkongers may still be seeing more ships flying the stars and stripes than they will of ships of the PLA navy, at least in the near future. The number of ship calls could turn out to be a barometer of the state of Sino-American relations.

*     *     *     *

An advance element of the People's Liberation Army moved into Hong Kong in late April. They were, per agreement, wearing uniforms, complete with the shoulder patches of the new Hong Kong garrison command, but carrying no weapons. Most local Hongkongers must have viewed them as so many aliens from outer space. Who knows what the soldiers privately thought of Hong Kong? Little information fed the frenzy of journalists as the Chinese troopers quickly disappeared inside of the Prince of Wales Barracks, headquarters of British Forces, in Central. They have not been seen again. About 200 more soldiers are anticipated before the handover date. The main body, of course, will move into Hong

Kong on July 1, apparently after daylight, so that it doesn't look like a night attack.

Meanwhile, half way up Victoria Peak, workmen are rushing to finish the gleaming, blue-green glass facade of the new building that will house the Chinese Foreign Ministry in Hong Kong. The structure, donated by tycoon Li Ka-shing, is on land once occupied by a building called the Hermitage that provided housing for civil servants. When I first came to Hong Kong, I lived across the street and used to walk over for some cheap meals at the restaurant on the upper floor. Presumably the Foreign Ministry's office will look after visiting dignitaries and coordinate with the various foreign consulates here. (One sticky question: the handful of offices from small countries that officially recognize Taiwan. Presumably, they will metamorphose into non-diplomatic "trade offices".) The main concern here seems to be whether the staff will provide employees for the consulates in the same way that the foreign ministry in Beijing vets the staff at foreign embassies there. The consulates would, of course, prefer to do their own hiring.

The Chinese, in fact, seem to have chosen their official representatives here with particular care. The Foreign Ministry reportedly is to be headed by an experienced diplomat, Jiang Enzhu, who was until January ambassador to Britain. The PLA deputy commander, Major-General Zhou Borong, who presumably will coordinate with the locals, is also fluent in English and was the first Chinese officer to attend the Royal Defence College. He is one of five Chinese generals in the garrison where the British made do with one. They include, of course, a political commissar. (When British garrison commander General Bryan Dutton asked Zhou why China was assigning five general officers to Hong Kong when the British made do with one, he replied, "Five Chinese generals are much cheaper than one British general.") But it is unknown who will head Xinhua after the handover, replacing the dour Communist Party *apparatchik,* Zhou Nan. He and his deputy plan to retire this year. The lack of a well-groomed successor contrasts with other key institutions and suggests confusion about the future status of this influential Beijing outpost in Hong Kong.

Both the new foreign office and the PLA garrison are rather straight-forward manifestations of the "one country" side of the famous formula, complementing existing institutions, such as the independent judiciary and the legislature on which the "two systems" part is based. Far more ambiguous is the future status of such established Beijing institutions as Xinhua, and the shadowy Hong Kong Work Committee, which is the main cover for the Chinese Communist Party in the colony.

Xinhua has a long history in Hong Kong. It was established in 1949, the year the People's Republic of China was founded. Since then it has been China's unofficial local representative and Beijing's eyes and ears in the colony. It is usually referred to as China's *de facto* consulate (although other agencies, such as the China Travel Service perform routine consular duties, such as issuing visas for tourists.) One might think that its mission will be over come the handover and that it will revert to its stated purpose as the local branch of the China's official news agency. Think again. Zhang Junsheng, the deputy director, told reporters in March that "Xinhua will continue to carry out the functions delegated by the central government. The director, ranking as a minister, will [continue] to be the most senior mainland official in Hong Kong."

That followed an article by prominent pro-China figure, Xu Simin, in *Wen Wei Po* arguing that Xinhua's major functions should be maintained. All of this seemed to suggest a strong underground campaign at work to preserve Xinhua, not to mention the jobs of approximately 600 people who work for it. One can easily imagine that some elements in Beijing would like to see Xinhua's vast network of contacts maintained. The local agency's influence is pervasive. It supports trade unions, the tenants' societies and such rural organizations as the Heung Yee Kuk in the New Territories, the body that officially represents Hong Kong's indigenous people. Xinhua also works closely with the traditional left-wing groups such as the pro-China schools, middle-class institutions like the

Chinese General Chamber of Commerce, and overt political parties like the Democratic Alliance for the Betterment of Hong Kong.

Xinhua at least operates pretty much openly. Not so the Chinese Communist Party. It too has a long pedigree in the colony, stretching back to the time before the war when communists organized dock strikes and later when it helped form guerrilla movements in the rural areas to harass Japanese occupiers. In the 1960s, when the Cultural Revolution convulsed China, the communists instigated local riots. It is understood that the director of Xinhua is the head of the local party apparatus. Most prominent leftists would deny being party members. The old colonial establishment never permitted communists to operate openly, but it never banned them either. Christine Loh has for some time been trying to clarify the party's status in law and even brought a motion to that effect to Legco. It was defeated by assembly president Andrew Wong's breaking a tied vote that divided along pro-democracy and pro-Beijing lines. It would appear that Beijing wants the communists to remain underground even after it resumes sovereignty. For example, although Hong Kong people have been appointed members of China's governmental bodies, such as the National People's Congress and the Chinese People's Political Consultative Conference for many years, there apparently will be no official Hong Kong delegation to the crucial 15th Congress of the Communist Party later this year.

Many people in Hong Kong, nevertheless, feel uneasy about Xinhua and the communists. In most Chinese cities, the party and government act in tandem. The leaders of the largest cities, Shanghai and Beijing, usually sit in the Politburo (it would be unusual to say the least if Tung, a dyed-in-the-wool capitalist, would take a seat in the party's top decision-making body). Tung himself has been rather circumspect in his comments about Xinhua's future, saying only that it is something to be decided by the central government. He has no reason to love an organization that worked strenuously for his leading rival, Yang Ti-liang, last year during the race for chief executive. But many believe that any "shadow governor" in Hong Kong pulling Tung's string will likely operate from behind the grim marble-faced walls of Xinhua's Happy Valley headquarters.

*       *       *       *

Tung stayed away from the gala opening of the new Tsing Ma suspension bridge, which links Lantau Island with the mainland. The spectacular span is just one element in the huge new airport complex at Chek Lap Kok. He supposedly had pressing business across the border, where he talked with officials in Guangdong province on ways to stop the influx of illegal child migrants. That is, of course, a serious matter, but Tung may also have found it expedient to be busy. The airport complex, after all, is not China's favorite construction project. It was billed specifically as a means of building confidence in the aftermath of Tiananmen, and a years-long, acrimonious dispute over funding from the Chinese who felt it not only was an expensive boondoggle and a nefarious British plot to drain the colony's coffers before they left poisoned relations between the two countries. The British would have liked to celebrate the grand opening of the airport, but, alas, that won't happen until 1998, so they had to make do with the bridge opening. They didn't spare their efforts. Former Prime Minister Margaret Thatcher came in to cut the ribbon. Helicopters carried a huge Union Jack overhead, bagpipers piped, fireworks burst. Britain's last hurrah. The Chinese press got back a subtle dig. The most common photograph of the ceremony was of Thatcher speaking, pictured against a blazing sunset.

# May 1997

*"Hong Kong is gripped by a greed-is-good mentality not seen in years."*

A LINE STRETCHED AROUND the block at the Causeway Bay branch of the Standard Chartered Bank. At first I thought it might be a run on the bank—it's happened before. Then I noticed security officials handing out forms. People were actually lining up for a chance to buy shares in Beijing Enterprises, which is going public next week. Interest is reaching a fever pitch. Beijing Enterprises is owned by the capital's municipal government and is far and away the hottest of the so-called "red chips"—Chinese enterprises listed on the Hong Kong Stock Exchange and raising capital in the colony.

This year has brought a host of offerings from companies with unfamiliar names—such as Shum Yip, Ng Fung Hong, Kinming Machine Tools—that have been snapped up by an eager public. Will they someday be as familiar as those Hong Kong blue chips, Jardines, Swire, the Hongkong and Shanghai Banking Corporation? Will their CEOs, people with Mandarin names such as Beijing Enterprises' Guo Yingming or Zhu Xiaohua, chairman of China Everbright-IHD, be as prominent in local business circles in the next ten years as Li Ka-shing or Gordon Wu?

All of these red-chip initial public offerings—IPOs—have been hugely oversubscribed. But nothing matched the feeding frenzy that gripped the colony in the last week of April. Housewives, taxi drivers, street hawkers—everyone it seemed—waited patiently in line to get their hands on the precious application forms. The underwriters initially printed about 400,000, and, as they were snapped up, put out a rush order for more. Some people offered to buy the forms off people ahead of them in line for HK$100, so anxious were they not to be left out. In the end, the issue was oversubscribed by 1,276 times; the average investor had about one chance in a thousand of actually being able to buy shares. The offering tied up US$27.5 billion for a week, twice the amount of cash normally circulating in the colony. Inter-banks rates shot up as money sloshed back and forth. For a week Beijing Enterprises held cash reserves larger than most foreign countries. And even after it distributed the refunds, it could still keep a windfall of about US$12 million in interest, equal to about half of the profits of the company the previous year.

Obviously the name "Beijing" had a magic quality. To the man-in-the-street this conjured strong *guanxi,* or big connections in the capital. It is sort of like being backed directly by the Federal Reserve System. That Chairman Hu Zhaoguang's was a Beijing vice mayor didn't hurt either. The company, in fact, seems to have some good assets, including the McDonalds' franchises in the capital and a monopoly on one of the segments of the Great Wall most popular with tourists. The lucky few who actually bought shares (most were reserved for investment houses) came out well. Offered at HK$12.48, they quickly climbed to HK$40.20 by the close of trading. The Hang Seng, Hong Kong's regular stock market index, has been climbing all year. Imagine what it would be doing if more than two red chips were on it. Some doomsayers, mostly in the Western media, claim that the bloom will go off red chips. Somehow it is part of the handover hysteria, and the promised Chinese state assets may not get "injected" into the Hong Kong holding companies, as expected. Or, they may turn out to be turkeys. Certainly something strange is operating when a company like China Everbright has its stock trading at 1,000 times 1996 earnings. "People who are rushing into the streets to try to pay HK$100 to get subscription forms may think they'll be able to sell at a big profit sometime soon, but things like that usually end up in tears, and it won't be any different this time," said investment analyst Kenneth Courtis visiting from Tokyo (and thus no stranger to stock and property bubbles).

The colony's generally buoyant mood reveals a manic side in the weeks preceding the handover. More than usual, it seems residents are gripped by what *Post* columnist Simon Pritchard called a "greed-is-good mentality not seen in the territory for years". In my neighborhood, parking lots are trading as if they were apartments with sea views. A flyer from my bank offers me "parking-lot loans". When the Heaven's Gate suicide was in the news a month or so ago with images of the cult's luxurious California mansion, swimming pool and tennis courts, the most common comment in Hong Kong was: "Oh, it's so cheap." Indeed, the US$1.6 million asking price is about the cost of a modest apartment here, no pool or tennis courts. People always call this a financial capital, but in my mind it often seems like Hong Kong's economy is nothing more than a highly sophisticated version of taking in each other's laundry. People put their savings into the stock market, take their profits out and buy property. They sell their apartments and put the proceeds back into stocks, in an ever upward spiral of asset inflation that seems bound to crash someday. I wonder to what extent the public's pre-handover confidence is based on what is essentially a financial house of cards. And if, sometime after July 1, it all comes crashing down, due to its own internal weaknesses and contradictions, will people draw the correct conclusions, or will they decide it is a failure of the handover?

\*   \*   \*   \*

A couple thousand of Hong Kong's social élite got letters three of four weeks ago telling them to keep their diaries free on the evenings of June 30 and July 1. For them it was the first hint that they might be among that select few, equally divided among friends of Britain and friends of China, invited to attend the big banquet that precedes the handover ceremony. They did not, of course, get the white embossed invitations bearing the royal coat of arms of Britain and the seal of China, looking like two families requesting the honor of your presence at the wedding of . . . two families who don't particularly like each other. So 4,000 or more guests are to be invited, but the two families are still haggling over the names. The tardiness in firming things up has complicated the social plans of many of Hong Kong's rich and famous, who weren't sure whether to delay their own plans to throw handover parties until they know whether they are among those invited to the Convention and Exhibition Centre. Naturally, anybody who is anybody, wants to be there, even though by all accounts it isn't likely to be as much fun as any one of 100 other bashes that will be going on simultaneously around town. Workmen are scrambling to finish the venues, the showcase US$620 million Convention and Exhibition Centre extension built on reclaimed land jutting into the harbor. It will be declared complete in time for the ceremony, even though the roof still leaked in one recent rainstorm, leaving big puddles where the guests of honor are supposed to sit. (The building's signature curved roofline is arresting but fraught with engineering complications.)

Imagine Washington on inauguration night. Multiply that by about a factor of ten, and you get an idea of what handover weekend will be like in Hong Kong: every restaurant booked, traffic in chaos, taxis impossible to obtain, buses, trams, ferries running through the night, even the airport open past its normal curfew in order to whisk the last remnants of the British Army back home. (For ten years it has been part of the Hong Kong legend that every hotel room would be filled. Apparently not. Perhaps the hotels gouged the prices just a bit too much. Some rooms are still available.) No fewer than two fireworks displays are planned, one British, one Chinese, with private yacht parties floating in the harbor to watch the pyrotechnics. All of the hotels are planning big parties. The biggest and boldest probably will be at the Regent, which modestly labels its parties the "Parties of the Century". On June 30, the hotel will be decorated with British colonial motif, with food and entertainment to match. At midnight it switches to a Chinese theme: The ballroom becomes the Forbidden City, silk and brocades appear everywhere, Chinese cuisine arrives from every corner of the Middle Kingdom. Celebrity chef Wolfgang Puck has been imported from the fashionable Los Angeles restaurant Sprago, popular with the Hollywood crowd. Cost per person, US$320.

On the flat expanse of concrete where the small naval basin at HMS *Tamar* used to be, tall aluminum stands have been erected for the spectators (chosen through a lottery system) who will attend the sunset festivities marking the end of British administration in the colony on June 30. Guests will listen to the bagpipes and massed bands of the Royal Marines, Scot's Guards, Black Watch and other British army units, all in all a very British affair. But the British do seem to be making a deliberate effort not to ruffle any Chinese sensitivities. Some people were even embarrassed to learn that Virgin Atlantic Airways was bringing in musicians to play a program of light classical and patriotic music called "Last Night of the Proms", (which might have been better called "Last Night of the Poms"). "Bawling out those undeniably British anthems is not the most sensitive way to celebrate the end of British rule," said the *Post* editorially. The Hong Kong Club's plans are also determinedly non-jingoistic. No crying or weeping at the stroke of midnight, says club chairman Stuart Leckie. Is it possible the British are playing things down too much? Who would begrudge them a few drunken rounds of *Rule Britannia* on their last night?

For a long time, the Chinese side was extremely coy about whom it would send. President Jiang Zemin was likely to come, but would he wait until after midnight to avoid sullying his feet on occupied soil? Finally in mid-June Xinhua released the names of the official delegation, headed, of course, by Jiang and Premier Li Peng and dozens of other notables. They will arrive shortly before midnight to witness the flag raising and to give a speech. Evidently, Jiang and company won't hang around for sight-seeing. The entourage plans to fly back to Beijing almost immediately where another celebratory banquet is planned at the Great Hall of the People. Big protocol problems have arisen over inaugural ceremonies installing the SAR government, which are to begin at I AM. American Secretary of State Madeleine Albright and British Prime Minister Tony Blair don't want to attend if it means standing and watching respectfully as the 60 members of the Provisional Legislature take their oaths. They plan to leave immediately after the handover. The Chinese have decided not to take this as a gross insult. A spokesman shrugged it off by saying that the guests are free to leave whenever they want to. "If the international audience wants to come, they will be welcome; but it won't be the same audience or the same room."

For many, the wee hours of July 1 will be the beginning of a working day. The Provisional Legislature is scheduled to go into session at 2:45 AM to pass a "reunification bill", putting the official stamp on all of the legislation they have been working on for the past four months. That includes the controversial amendments to the Public Order Ordinance requiring police notification and permits for demonstrations. No doubt, Tung will stay awake long enough to put his chop on it too. That will leave a window of a few hours, in which, presumably, lawlessness will prevail. How will the Democrats and other protesters fill them? The Democrats, at least, have begun to show their hand. No, they won't chain themselves to their legislative desks. But they say they will enter the Legco building at around 10 PM on June 30. If they are blocked, they have hinted at some kind of civil disobedience. Martin Lee will deliver a manifesto from the north balcony, presumably to an audience consisting to a large degree of foreign members of the media. It promises to be a long night.

\*       \*       \*       \*

Tung seems to be displaying a little more political dexterity in his dealings with Beijing these days. The proposed electoral arrangements for the first post-1997 Legco were made final by the Preparatory Committee at its (presumably) last meeting May 25–26. The committee wanted to recommend a single vote, multi-member method of voting (which would guarantee that the runners-up, usually pro-Beijing candidates, would get elected). But rather than accept the committee's decision, Tung seems to have said to Beijing's leaders: "give me some options". After all, it is he and not the committee that took the political pounding over the civil liberties ordinances, even though the decision came from Beijing. He is also resisting a proposal engineered by Xinhua to create a new functional constituency for "Chinese-funded enterprises" as one of those replacing the old Patten-designed districts. One could argue, of course, that red chips are indeed playing an increasing role in Hong Kong's economy, but it was probably a rather blatant effort to get a Legco seat for Communist Party cadres disguised as corporate directors.

Tung prefers a system of proportional representation (PR) for that segment of the new Legco returned through direct elections. That would be a lot easier to sell overseas, since numerous democracies in Europe have PR and many political scientists argue that it is a fairer and more democratic election method than first-past-the-post, as employed in 1995. That argument might resonate stronger, however, if the *entire* Legco were elected by PR and not just one-third. Basically, Beijing wants the Democrats to participate in the upcoming legislative election because it will give the first SAR legislature a sense of legitimacy. It just doesn't want to be embarrassed again by having them sweep the board. What will result is a Legco looking a lot more like the Macau Legislative Assembly, which operates under a PR system. In Macau (it doesn't have political parties as such) no individual group comes close to dominating the assembly.

\*     \*     \*     \*

Fresh trouble on the "dream team?" The colony has been buffeted by a spate of gossip that Chief Secretary Anson Chan, the head of the civil service, and the chief executive-designate, surprise, surprise, do not see eye to eye on many issues, including political values and government appointments. In an interview published in *Newsweek,* the chief secretary hinted that she was prepared to quit if the SAR administration's policies and her principles clashed. The next day Tung's special adviser, Paul Yip, told the Chinese-language newspaper *Ming Pao* that Chan would just have to adjust her thinking to the new political realities. Unlike Patten, who delegated near-complete administrative authority to Chan and the other top civil servants, Tung would be a "hands-on" chief executive, "with his own views and sense of responsibilities," Yip said. Of course, the two never had much in common. Tung chose to keep Anson, and the rest of the senior civil servants, because it was considered essential for confidence. Hong Kong citizens needed to experience some semblance of a through-train in the civil service. (The possibilities of change after the handover increase. Financial Secretary Donald Tsang, for example, was on the Queen's Knight's list in May.) But Tung's people never really trusted Chan, who is, after all, steeped in the culture of Britain's Colonial Service. Tung is a conservative former business executive with little experience in government aside from a rather quiet four-year stint on Patten's Executive Council.

Tung has been in a curious limbo, not exactly a leader-in-waiting, but not fully vested with authority either. In some respects, he is doing the kind of thing expected of any leader living through the lag between selection and inauguration. Like the US President-elect, he is putting his new government together, appointing officials. In Late May he named respected Queen's Counsel Andrew Li as his choice to become the first post-1997 chief justice. It was widely applauded, even though Li, the scion of the influential Bank of East Asia clan whose members include one losing candidate for chief executive, Simon Li, has relatively little experience on the bench. But in other respects, Tung is already governing. When the crisis over illegal child immigrants flared earlier this year, it was he, not Patten, who went across the border to discuss matters with Guangdong Province authorities. Even his decision to live in his own private apartment rather than Government House and to work out of the Central Government Offices has symbolic overtones. It underscores that Tung is not just another in a long line of British colonial governors. He is the head of an entirely new political entity to be born on July 1. (So what to do with Government House? Suggestions range from turning it into a museum of colonial horrors, a guest house for visiting dignitaries, or a place for special events, as with the Akasaka detached palace in Tokyo.)

\*     \*     \*     \*

I went down to Victoria Park to watch the candlelight vigil in memory of the June 4 crackdown. It was the first I had attended since the dramatic moment eight years ago when people by the tens of thousands—a million it was said, and it could be true—marched solemnly through the streets of Hong Kong Island. They wore black and white, the traditional mourning colors, still in shock after learning of the swift, massive show of armed might in Beijing the previous night. The memorial takes place on what passes for Hong Kong's own Tiananmen Square, an expanse the size of six soccer fields at the south end of Victoria Park, where the bronze statue of Queen Victoria sits at the entrance looking placidly towards the mountains. A more appropriate, although less permanent, monument had been placed in the center of the fields. It was an eight-meter tall concrete stele of 50 twisted, agonizing bodies by the Danish sculptor Jens Galschiøt, called the "Pillar of Shame". The Alliance wants to erect it permanently somewhere but hasn't been able to obtain permission. Hong Kong University authorities waffled over it, after the statue was removed to university grounds, and a brief altercation broke out after students tried to have it put on permanent display. They seem to have settled on a compromise so that it will remain there, at least through September.

Shortly after dark the field was already filling up, and more people streamed in from the subway station exits on either side of the park. They were ordinary Hongkongers, looking as if they had come directly from work. They sat quietly in neat rows, holding their paper candlestick holders, waiting to listen to the speakers.

Hawkers in mobile carts sold small plastic replicas of the Goddess of Democracy and other souvenirs. A large knot of people clustered around a figure whom I could barely make out and did not recognize. Some famous dissident or "black hand"? (the Chinese term for Tiananmen agitators), I asked one of the Chinese journalists standing by, and she casually replied, "I think he's going to burn himself." Rumors had circulated of a self-immolation. It didn't take place.

The Hong Kong Alliance in Support of the Patriotic Democratic Movements in China obviously pulled out the stops to make this year's observances unforgettable. As early as March it had set up booths in the subway stations handing out literature. On the Sunday prior to June 4, a large group carrying black and white banners demonstrated outside of Xinhua demanding that an accounting be made, dissidents released and perpetrators brought to justice. Until last year the observances had been dwindling in numbers. Attendance rebounded last year over concerns that by this time the traditional venues might have been booked for happy handover events. In fact, pro-Beijing people did try to block the memorial by reserving the park for a soccer tournament. Evidently the government pressured the Urban Council to let the Alliance have its traditional venue to hold observances.

The unanswered question on everybody's mind: is this the last one? In an interview in the *Asian Wall Street Journal* last October, Foreign Minister Qian Qichen had said that such activities had best be dropped. In a more recent interview in June with the *Post,* however, he seemed to soften his remarks, saying they were his "personal opinion". Tung has said the events should be allowed to continue so long as people obey the law (and considering the utter peacefulness of such events, I could see no possible grounds for the police to deny a permit). He seemed compelled, however, to say that Hong Kong people should "set aside" memories of Tiananmen and look to the future. Many people in the park were defiantly promising that they will be back next year even if the demonstration is technically banned, even if it meant they had to resort to civil disobedience.

The tone of this year's memorial seems to have changed subtly. Few if any strident voices called out "Down with Li Peng" or any other Chinese leader. The main message was never to forget. Szeto Wah said, "As long as there are Chinese in this world, June 4 will not be forgotten ... as long as June 4 is remembered, it will be redressed." For its part, Xinhua's ritual denunciation in the official media sounded a bit perfunctory. And in Beijing some signs of a reassessment may be emerging slowly. During his funeral oration for Deng Xiaoping last February, President Jiang referred to the protests in Tiananmen Square as "disturbances" in striking contrast with the official designation of "counter-revolutionary riot". For that matter, "counter-revolution" is no longer a part of China's official vocabulary, thanks to a new criminal code passed by the National People's Congress in March. To be sure, the authorities still have plenty of tools left to suppress any threats to state security, but it does move China along from a state defined in purely Marxist terms of class dictatorship toward a more civil society. Student protesters will not suddenly be called heroes of democracy rather than counter-revolutionaries, but perhaps it is possible to imagine they might some day be called what they always proclaimed themselves to be—patriots.

# June 30, 1997

*"I have relinquished the administration of this Government.
God Save the Queen."*

THE LAST HUMID DAYS of June were filled with alarums and excursions, excitement, and after thirteen years of anticipation, perhaps some ennui also. Those for whom the handover weekend would be one long party filled the shops looking for appropriate clothes. Chinese garments were certainly in; that irrepressible self-promoter, David Tang, organized something called "Dress Chinese Day". Ostensibly to help raise money for the Community Chest, it was scheduled for July 3, the first working day after the handover. In an interview on BBC, he allowed that while, of course, many fine places sell Chinese clothes in Hong Kong, few match the quality of his own downtown emporium, Shanghai Tang. (Tang's burst of patriotism did not prevent his accepting an OBE from the British in the last honors list, published in mid-June.)

In Aberdeen Harbour the fishing boats flew red Chinese flags and the new banner of post-1997 Hong Kong, a red field with a white bauhinia flower in the center of it. But *The Opium War,* the Chinese movie made in Shanghai with the handover in mind depicting how the perfidious British obtained Hong Kong, first by stuffing China with opium then bombarding its weak forts, opened in mid-June. It didn't seem to pull in many viewers. The cinema was practically empty when I saw the film. Admittedly, it was a Friday afternoon on a working day, but it certainly was not packing them in like the new dinosaur epic, *The Lost World,* which also opened here in late June.

Thousands of journalists descended and began poking around the city looking for stories. For a while the press pack, tantalized by the news of Cambodian mass-murderer Pol Pot's apparent capture, hurried off to Phnom Penh. But the reporters drifted back to Hong Kong when it became apparent that he wasn't about to emerge from the jungle. In the last week before the handover, it seemed impossible to walk around Central without running into a minicam. Chan Ah-ho, one of Hong Kong's notorious cage people, had her fifteen minutes of fame, as, one by one, foreign television journalists and cameramen squeezed their equipment up the narrow hallway steps and into her flophouse. A local welfare and human rights group took so many camera crews through Chan's place that there seemed to be more reporters than cage dwellers. I'm not so sure of the numbers of these unfortunate folks. The tally of visiting journalists: 6,421 officially accredited. "This will be the most over-reported event of the century," complained Heung Shu-fai, a Chinese news media executive.

The Legislative Council went into session one last week before being disbanded. A curiosity of this assembly is how active a role non-elected civil servants play in the legislative process. When I took my seat in the visitor's gallery one afternoon, the members were debating a copyright bill. The Secretary for Trade and Industry, Denise Yue, was lecturing the legislators on the deficiencies of certain amendments. "It would be irrational to support the honorable member's bill," she said forthrightly in clipped British English. I wonder if this is what people mean when they say that Hong Kong has a strong "executive-led" government? In fact, Legco passed quite a lot of socially progressive legislation in its dying days, including one of the world's strongest ordinances restricting the advertising and marketing of cigarettes, an ordinance granting workers in Hong Kong the right to bargain collectively and legislator Christine Loh's private-member's bill restricting the government's ability to reclaim land from the harbor. Legco finally wound up its business after a last all-night session at 8 AM on June 29. Accompanied by tears, bear hugs and promises to return, Hong Kong's most democratic legislature passed into history.

The question, of course, was what would they do next? Ever since the Chinese promised to dismantle Legco nearly two years ago and replace it with a temporary one of its own choosing, many people have wondered how the ousted Democrats would react on handover night. Would they barricade themselves in the chamber or chain themselves to their desks and invite the police to come in and drag them out in the full view of the world's media? The temptation would was surely be strong. Of course, such extreme civil disobedience had never really seemed in character. By and large, Hong Kong's politicians are too law-abiding—and too fastidious—to bash heads with the police. Speaking to a group of journalists in May, Martin Lee joked, "I told [Democratic whip] Szeto Wah not to chain himself to his desk. Frankly, what would you do if you had to go to the bathroom?" That was his way of saying that, whatever they might have planned for the night of June 30, it wasn't going to be radical.

That no confrontation was likely to occur became clearer when, in mid-June, they finally revealed their hand. After attending the handover ceremony (because the party supports the return of Hong Kong to China), Lee and a half-a-dozen colleagues would return to the Legco building and deliver a manifesto from the second-story balcony overlooking the war memorial. All through the week, the Democrats negotiated with the Tung administration and the provisional legislature, winning grudging permission to enter the building after midnight, but not to use the balcony for any speeches. It is not clear why Tung and his advisers were so set against allowing the Democrats to speak their piece from the balcony, although he did say, "This is supposed to be a happy day for the people of China and for Chinese people all over the world. Nothing will spoil the happiness of this particular occasion."

Britain's effort, meanwhile, to demonstrate solidarity with the outgoing Legco by boycotting the swearing-in of the incoming provisional council seems to have failed. Only US Secretary of State Madeleine Albright agreed to join Prime Minister Tony Blair in giving the investiture a miss. Every other country, including such bastions of democracy as Australia, Canada and Japan, indicated they planned to send their most senior people to both the handover and the swearing-in ceremony that takes place about one hour later. So London climbed down. Blair would still stay away but Britain's new consul general in Hong Kong, Francis Cornish, would attend; after all, he has to live with these people. Washington promptly fell in line by assigning Consul General Richard Boucher to the ceremony. *Post* cartoonist Paul Best summed things up best by depicting the British and American leaders falling through a foot bridge labeled "the moral high ground". In fact, Blair is probably only too eager to put the past confrontation behind him. During his brief stay, he arranged a private meeting with Jiang Zemin.

One week before the handover, I went to the Lok Ma Chau lookout to check out the bridge over which the People's Liberation Army garrison will pass when it enters Hong Kong on July 1. Back when China was closed to almost all outsiders, this was a popular tourist place. People came to gaze across the border into what was then a deeply mysterious "Red China". Now in a few days Red China is coming to Hong Kong.

It was never exactly a military secret that the PLA would move several thousand troops into Hong Kong sometime on July 1, across this bridge and at several other crossing points. But it seemed that in the days immediately preceding the handover, the colony experienced a fresh attack of jitters about it. One reason was the curious last-minute Chinese demand that additional troops besides the 200 already in the advance party be allowed to enter Hong Kong before midnight. Why was never completely clear, aside from the official reason that they had to be there to perform their stated "defensive duties" as the clock struck twelve. The British strenuously argued against the advance deployment on sovereignty grounds but eventually agreed to let exactly 509 soldiers enter Hong Kong at 9 PM on June 30. They could bring in their weapons—464 to be precise, with exactly 150 rounds of ammunition each—but the guns had to be "licensed" and locked in carrying crates until midnight. Britain's position was weak, since the Chinese with equal logic could have demanded that every single British soldier be out of their territory by 00:01 AM, a physical impossibility. In the end, it may well have come down to nothing more than symmetry, the first battalion of PLA troops entering Hong Kong three hours before midnight, the last 500 or so Tommies departing from Kai Tak Airport at around 3:30 AM. The Chinese are particular about such things.

Added to the anxiety was the Chinese penchant for withholding details of their movements until the last moment. Even one week before the handover, Franco Kwok, Assistant District Officer for the Northern New Territories, told me he was in the dark about their movements. He didn't know if the communist troops would come into Hong Kong in trucks, in buses or marching behind a brass band. Some of the rural associations had planned to lay on a welcoming ceremony for the troops as they passed through. Soft drinks were on hand to pass out, pigs ready to be roasted. But even they couldn't nail down exactly where or when the PLA would enter. So the official announcement about three days before the handover explaining exactly how many troops would enter and from what border points seemed to some to be unduly provocative. The *New York Times* wrote that the "decision" (as if it had been made yesterday) to garrison 4,000 troops in Hong Kong was a "crude move to intimidate citizens".

Hong Kong people have long been nervous that the PLA might be used to suppress demonstrations or that they might in any way hold themselves up to be above local laws. The news that the garrison planned to bring in a small squadron of wheeled armored personnel carriers, looking suspiciously like they might be designed more for crowd control than defense, didn't allay tensions either. The PLA high command knows about these concerns and has said on several occasions that it hopes to use the garrison to change the army's negative image. It has work to do. In the weeks preceding the handover a couple of small incidents, including one in which the deputy garrison commander, General Zhou Borong, was accused of bad manners in a small border crossing altercation (concerning whether he had the right license plate) also raised anxiety levels. That incident apparently was caused by language (Mandarin versus Cantonese) problems. Some complaints were made about the PLA canceling a public bus stop near the old Stanley Fort too. The Chinese language media in Hong Kong pounce on every gaffe. "On the public relations front, the PLA is fighting an uphill battle," wrote political commentator Andy Ho. In fact, the PLA garrison is to be, in size and types of weapons, quite similar to the British army's posture as recently as 1994. But last-minute delays, surprises and plain misrepresentation all conspired to keep the troops in the headlines through the last week.

*       *       *       *

On handover day, June 30, I got up early and went down to Central to watch while, at 7 AM, three kilted soldiers of the Black Watch regiment raised for the last time the British service flags on the war memorial that dominates Statue Square. The small green patch that surrounds the war memorial was lined with tourists and a few journalists. Old colonial rituals such as this one drew large crowds all day. About 300 people witnessed the firing of the Noon-Day Gun (not, in this case, for the last time).

I often wondered what will happen to the Cenotaph and the few other British monuments, such as the big bronze statue of Queen Victoria in her park. I doubt that the Chinese will imme-diately tear them down as symbols of hated European colonialist oppression, as Russians pulled down statues to Karl Marx or Vladimir Lenin. I don't sense that kind of pent-up anger, and, in any case, it would make the new SAR look bad. The long-time campaigner for veterans' benefits, Jack Edwards, once told me he hopes that the war memorial will remain since the British and Chinese fought in a common cause during World War II. That's probably wishful thinking. Maybe for a few years the British consul general will lay a wreath on Remembrance Day. But eventually, in

a very Hong Kong way, the memorial will disappear in some kind
of waterfront redevelopment project. This is Hong Kong. What
would people rather have on that precious space, a 30-story building or an old concrete block?

In the afternoon I went to listen as Martin Lee held forth before
a large contingent of visiting journalists at the Foreign Correspondents' Club. He was in fine form. A reporter from Prague asked
him what he felt about the PLA moving in tomorrow. He replied:
"That's an appropriate question coming from you. They just want
to intimidate people with a demonstration of force to show who
is boss." Lee said he had worked out a simple contingency plan
should the authorities try to stop him from speaking from the
balcony. He would simply scramble up by a ladder. "I know that
some of you are taking bets on whether I can climb to the second
story in one minute."

From the FCC, I trudged up the hill to Government House.
Already the threatening skies had turned into a steady drizzle. By
the time I got there, Chris Patten had already taken his final salute,
made three circuits of the driveway in his official car (a Chinese
custom signifying a desire to return one day) and driven the short
distance to the former HMS *Tamar* for Britain's sunset farewell. A
small crowed still lingered outside the gates, which continue to
bear the large EIIR. A young Chinese man holding a Hong Kong
colonial flag displayed a sign that read, I'LL REMEMBER U, MR PATTEN.
Presumably he meant fondly. Indeed, a considerable amount of
goodwill for Britain's 28th and last governor of Hong Kong was
evident all through the day. Patten's last public approval rating was
79 percent.

I was tempted to stay behind in Statue Square in the gathering
rain and hear Martin Lee's speech from the Legco balcony, but in
the end I went home. It was obviously going to be impossible to
take in everything from one vantage point, so I decided to do what
millions of other Hongkongers would be doing—watch it on
television. From that medium and from talking with colleagues

who deployed throughout the colony that night, I got the following unforgettable impressions:

- Of the British farewell parade as the bagpipers and army bands
  wheeled and saluted, seemingly oblivious to the pouring rain.
  Organizers of the last good-bye had threatened to call things
  off if it rained. It did, but they didn't. Only a typhoon would
  have stopped this show. Where the sun should have been
  drooping on the horizon was a black wall of storm clouds so
  thick that hardly any light penetrated. End of Empire? More
  like the end of the world. A stoic Prince Charles soldiered on
  as the rain drenched his white-dress navy uniform and turned
  his notes into mush. The other dignitaries huddled under their
  canopies and umbrellas, like boy scouts on a wet and soggy
  weekend camping trip.

- Of Chris Patten making his graceful last speech as governor—
  "Now Hong Kong people are to run Hong Kong. It is their
  unshakable destiny"—and the enduring applause that followed, obliging him to return to the podium for a bow and a
  wave. He appeared jaunty, but several times he noticeably bit
  his lip. When he took his seat, he bowed his head as if hiding
  tears. They were certainly not the first nor the last for the day.
  Many among the spectators—about half Chinese, the rest
  expatriate—linked arms and gazed sorrowfully at the ground.

- Of the military precision of the short but certainly "solemn
  and dignified" midnight handover ceremony itself. Every detail,
  from the exact size of the flags to the moment when the
  "principal representatives" took their seats, had been ham-
  mered out in mind-numbing negotiating sessions. Everything
  was timed right down to the last second. The British anthem,
  *God Save the Queen,* absolutely had to end no later than five
  seconds before midnight, the Chinese insisted. It did.

- Of the moderation exhibited by China's President Jiang Zemin, who declined an opportunity to gloat over reclaiming what the Chinese had always believed was rightfully their territory, Instead, he promised to maintain Hong Kong's autonomy and spoke of a time when the new region would "gradually develop a democratic system that suits Hong Kong's reality". Returning to his seat, he seemed to wave to someone in the VIP box. I like to think it was to Zhou Lin, the widow of the late patriarch Deng Xiaoping, architect of "one country, two systems", who attended the handover ceremony with one of her daughters.

- Of the eloquence of Martin Lee as he spoke from the Legco balcony surrounded by many of his Democratic colleagues (they didn't need a ladder to climb up, after all, no doubt disappointing the hordes of journalists hoping to record what would have been the only unrehearsed event of the evening), calling July 1 a "glorious day" for all Chinese people and promising that he and his party would stay in the new SAR and continue to "defend the freedoms we cherish. The flame of democracy has been ignited and is burning in the hearts of our people; it will not be extinguished. We say to all of you gathered here and to Hong Kong's friends around the world: We shall return."

- Of the awkwardness of some members of Hong Kong's new government when, in the early hours of July 1, they took their oaths of office in Mandarin, the national language, rather than in Cantonese, the local dialect. Executive Councillor Chung Sze-yeun's heavy accent even elicited a titter of laughter. Incoming Chief Justice Andrew Li started off in Mandarin, but rather wisely switched to English. The judges in their red gowns and white wigs, however, were a reminder of the continuity of English common law and liberties in Hong Kong even in this most Chinese of settings.

- Of the loud cheers and quiet tears of many ordinary Hong Kong people and former colonials as the British flags were lowered and the flag of China and the new SAR banner were raised. "I'm very happy to be welcoming China, but I'm a little worried for our future," said a Kowloon taxi driver. "You feel the whole world moved underneath you," said Gina Shannon, a British resident. "It's not Hong Kong anymore."

- And, finally, of the poignant farewell at Tamar, the Royal Yacht *Britannia* bathed in the white glow of giant light globes, Patten slowly working his way through a crowd of old friends and colleagues, stopping for a kiss here, for a bear hug there, his three daughters, eyes glistening but heads held high, crossing onto the yacht, the strains of *Rule Britannia* as the ship gradually pulled away from the dock and steamed slowly eastward through the Lei Yue Mun gap, Patten and the Prince waving good-bye from the upper deck.

- The last message from *Britannia* – For the Secretary of State from the Governor of Hong Kong: I have relinquished the administration of this Government. God Save the Queen.

# Epilogue: July 1997

*"A new era, a new identity."*

THEY EMERGED THROUGH THE MIST like ghosts, another small flotilla of patrol boats and their support vessels, this time from the Chinese Navy. The dark gray of the hulls provided a perfect camouflage against the sodden sky and persistent rain. Only the bright red ensigns provided a splash of color. They had slipped away from their bases in the Pearl River Delta well before dawn to cross into Hong Kong waters at precisely 6 AM, chugging under the new Tsing Ma Bridge and heading for their berths at Stonecutters Island, just vacated by the Royal Navy. At Lok Ma Chau and two other border crossings, trucks carrying People's Liberation Army soldiers began to move as the first signs of sunlight leaked through the dark clouds. The soldiers sat ramrod straight in their trucks, weapons slung across their shoulders, as the rain poured down. Along the way a few children lined the road to wave red flags in greeting. The troops did not stop but disappeared into the new barracks.

It rained continuously for a week after the inauguration of the new Special Administrative Region. Several celebratory parades had to be canceled. Landslides closed sections of Castle Peak Road. The chief executive's office issued a statement saying it was watching the situation carefully. Police and other safety services, regardless of what badge they now wore, came out in their rain slicks to direct traffic and take the injured to hospitals, just as they always do. The heavy rains were strangely reassuring. From the unknown hazards of the future, attention was quickly diverted to the more familiar, everyday hazards of life in Hong Kong. The Chinese and SAR flags—flying from the hotels and banks and the Prince of Wales barracks, now PLA headquarters—were almost the only sign of change. Three ROC flags hung defiantly at the entrance to Ap Lei Chau Island. In the courts British judges continued to dispense justice, still addressed by lawyers as "your worship". The city had an air of normalcy.

The new chief executive, Tung Chee-hwa, maintained a hectic pace, appearing tired at times but also seeming to relish the excitement and the power. He grabbed a few hours sleep after his swearing-in, then plunged back into the whirlwind. The Buddhists, celebrating the founding of the SAR with a mass rally at the stadium, wanted to extend their personal blessing. He gave them 90 seconds. Local Canadians celebrated their July 1 national day; he dropped by to join them. On July 2, he held his first press conference. The contrast with the past was evident. Veteran reporter Jonathan Mirsky of *The Times* of London often asked the opening question during Patten's time. He was kept waiting. Tung responded in smooth English, Cantonese or Mandarin, depending on the language of the question. Some watching his performance closely noted that he seemed to adopt the communist-style of clapping himself at pre-ordained moments. But the fact that he held a press conference two days into his tenure seemed a sign that he wanted to continue the policies of open government initiated by his British predecessor. Will he follow Patten's example and submit himself to questions from legislators once a month?

The provisional legislature had hardly occupied the chambers vacated by the outgoing Legco than it set about, at the behest of the government, undoing some of its predecessor's work. Anson Chan moved to suspend for several months seven laws passed during the last legislature's dying days, most of them relating to labor rights. It seemed to many as if big business was still calling the shots. The provisionals also adopted the government's proposal requiring mainland-born children of Hong Kong residents to obtain something called a "certificate of entitlement" before being allowed to settle in Hong Kong. The Tung administration claimed that this action was necessary to keep the social services from being swamped with migrants; lawyers argued that it was already playing loose with the region's new constitution, which rather clearly grants these children the right to live in the SAR. On a mid-July Sunday, some 500 labor activists and democrats rallied at the Star Ferry pier and marched to Tung's offices half-a-mile uphill carrying banners and chanting slogans. Union leader Lee Cheuk-yan staged a hunger strike to protest the re-emergence of pro-business values. "Hong Kong is entering the dark ages," he proclaimed. Maybe; but from my perspective, the new Hong Kong looked and felt a lot like the old Hong Kong.

\*   \*   \*   \*

Still, in his inaugural speech July 1, Tung Chee-hwa proclaimed the beginning of "a new era, a new identity", seeming to suggest that Hong Kong was entering unfamiliar waters. For the present he promised to tackle one of the SAR's most pressing social problems, lack of affordable housing, by making more land available, streamlining the development process and curbing rampant speculation. He set an ambitious goal: building 85,000 new homes a year. Almost immediately, the new Citizens Party, led by liberal ex-legislator Christine Loh, criticized the proposals as too little too late. "Until the chief executive puts specific time frames on these promises, they remain empty ones," she said. Anyone who thought that politics was something Chris Patten carried home with him in his baggage would be disabused of that notion quickly. Unlike the mainland, Hong Kong has a political opposition. While many opposition politicians are currently out of office, they show no signs of disappearing or being cowed by Hong Kong's changed circumstances.

No matter what the democrats may say in their flights of rhetoric about the end of democracy, the end of civil liberties, the end of the rule of law, they don't act like they believe it. In fact, many prominent people of all political persuasions have made important personal decisions, based on the assumption that they can pursue a political career post-1997. Pro-Beijing legislator David

Chu gave up his American passport because he felt it would be a handicap in the new politics. DAB chairman Tsang Yok-sing recently quit his job as principal of Pui Kiu to devote himself full-time to elective politics. As reported earlier, Peter Woo gave up many of his corporate positions in his quest to be chief executive. He is certainly behaving as if he might run for that office again. Christine Loh also talks about giving up her British passport because she feels it inappropriate for a politician in China (her words) to be technically a foreigner (even though the Basic Law allows a minority of foreign passport holders to sit in the legislature).

Indeed, Loh and her fellow Citizens are already looking past even the first post-1997 election, probably in May 1998, to a time when the government may be chosen entirely through elections. The Basic Law holds out the prospect that after 2007 Hong Kong may choose its chief executive through direct elections as well as its entire legislature (such an eventuality, however, would still require the approval of China's National People's Congress). So the dissidents have set their sights on a time in the not-too-distant future when they might contest all 60 seats of the assembly. Loh's goal for her Citizens Party is nothing less than to become Hong Kong's "ruling party".

To be debated endlessly is the extent to which this political awakening was Chris Patten's doing. Certainly, on one level his political reforms must be considered a failure. After all, the Chinese simply disbanded his elected legislature and replaced it with one of its own choosing. That body is writing new electoral rules so that the next legislature will be a more conservative body. Remember, however, that Patten's reforms were, for all the controversy, pretty conservative. Even the former governor admitted as much an a farewell interview with the *South China Morning Post*: "I'm constantly amazed at how a set of very modest proposals on elections were built up into . . . a sort of maniacal struggle for the very soul of democracy in Asia." His latest line is that his electoral system, though now dismantled, at least gave more than a million people in Hong Kong the experience of participating in a fair, open and honest election. They will now want to repeat the experience. That argument rather conveniently ignores the fact that nearly a million people participated in a fair, open and honest election the year before he arrived. And yet, his proposition may contain an element of truth. I always felt that one reason why the election for the chief executive came to resemble a general election, even though the franchise was so narrow, was because of the governor. Nobody would admit it for a minute, of course, but it always appeared to me that the candidates were consciously or unconsciously copying the Patten style.

\* \* \* \*

In mid-July, the Tung administration issued instructions to the police, giving them discretionary powers to ban political protests in Hong Kong that impinge on "national security". It was putting some teeth in the controversial amendments to the Public Order and Societies ordinances that so roiled the colony before the handover. Despite this, I remain cautiously optimistic that most of Hong Kong's treasured civil liberties will survive the transition. I don't think that Beijing's leaders care that much what freedoms Hong Kong people enjoy, so long as exercising them does not undercut their own position in China. Hong Kong people can march down Queen's Road every day—they practically do that already—so long as they don't "interfere" with the internal politics of mainland China. The difficulty? Many people in Hong Kong do want to "interfere" in China. And as Hong Kong gradually becomes more closely a part of China—as people increasingly feel their own identity is tied to the mainland and its future—they will naturally desire a more active role in their country's affairs.

The former dissident Han Dongfang, the last Tiananmen activist in Hong Kong, continues to fight for independent labor unions and democracy in China from his home on Lamma Island. Han writes the *China Labor Bulletin,* which is broadcast on Radio Free Asia and mailed as a newsletter to the mainland each month.

Christians of all denominations often feel morally bound to "interfere" in China, too. Conservative evangelicals give their support to the so-called underground churches and sometimes help smuggle Bibles into China. Their more liberal counterparts support such groups as the Christian Industrial Committee, advocating labor rights and attacking sweat-shops among the Hong Kong–owned business across the border. Newspaper editors can hardly avoid "interfering" when they publish news, analysis and commentary about Chinese affairs. They cannot confine their reporting to Hong Kong alone; their readers have come to expect honest, comprehensive reporting on China. Martin Lee dreams openly of a time when he may be able to advocate democracy not just from the rather narrow confines of a small legislature in one Chinese city but someday in the Great Hall of the People as an *elected* member of China's National People's Congress.

If one side of the "Hong Kong system" may come under severe strain in the near future, it may be not in politics or even civil liberties, but the economy. On the surface, it would seem that big business is firmly in control. After all, the new chief executive is the scion of a wealthy shipping family who worked his whole adult life in business. His major patron in the race for chief executive was billionaire property tycoon, Li Ka-shing. He was chosen not by popular election but by a 400-member electoral college, whose members, though nominally drawn from all sectors of society, were in fact tilted heavily toward the business élite. In his July 1 speech, Tung paid glowing tribute to Hong Kong's free-market system. "Hong Kong is at present the freest and most vibrant economy in the world. Free enterprise and free trade, prudent fiscal management and low taxation; the rule of law, an executive-led government and an efficient civil service have been part of our tradition."

He then went on to signal a desire for more active government with special emphasis on such things as improving education and social welfare for the aged and more active intervention in the marketplace to curb speculation and bring down property prices. "We have to resolve a series of social problems arising from a growing and aging population, meet the pressing demand for more and better housing and deal with employment dislocation due to restructuring of the economy," he said. "Beneath the surface of prosperity, there are insidious threats, which are taxing our courage and determination."

Social pressures are compelling attention as never before. They may not be resolved through traditional means. The plight of immigrant children is just one sign of a rapidly growing and changing population. Government forecasts now expect a 30 percent increase in Hong Kongs' population over the next 20 years, from six million to about ten million. Add to this other demographic shifts, such as a maturing population, soaring property prices, eroding industrial base, and it is clear that many of the older prescriptions may not suffice.

Some of Tung's advisers feel strongly that the government should also take a more active role in economic planning. That means to choose economic winners and weed out losers, copying some of the recent industrial development policies of Taiwan, Malaysia, Japan and Singapore. Many would claim that this is tampering dangerously with the elements that have made Hong Kong so successful. Some will take it as *prima facie* evidence that, as soon as the British had departed, the place began to go downhill. Others might argue that the new administration was simply facing up to needs and new challenges left unresolved by the departing colonialists.

It is now nearly two decades since the late Chinese patriarch Deng Xiaoping coined the phrase, *gangren zhigang*, literally meaning, "Hong Kong people ruling Hong Kong". This most assuredly did not apply to the 143 years that preceded the signing in 1984 of the Sino-British Joint Declaration governing the return of the colony to China. Before then, no pretense was made that Hong Kong people governed themselves. Hong Kong was a British crown colony administered by governors appointed in London with near absolute powers. Nor can it be said that Hong Kong people ruled themselves during the thirteen years between the signing of the

Joint Declaration and the handover at midnight June 30. Even the local budget for 1997/98 was thrashed out by Chinese and British diplomats behind closed doors.

As the handover date approached, China's hand in shaping the future Special Administrative Region became more apparent, some might say heavy. First came an *ad hoc* group called the Preliminary Working Committee, formed to bridge the impasse over Governor Chris Patten's political reforms. It was superseded by the Preparatory Committee, made up of people from Hong Kong and China but chosen by Beijing. That body was responsible for creating the SAR's first political institutions, notably the selection of the chief executive. China's paramount concerns were evident in the committee's unpopular decisions to scrap the elected Legco and to recommend invalidating sections of the Societies and Public Order ordinances and the Bill of Rights.

But the handover and the birth of the SAR have cleared the decks. For the first time, Hong Kong people will be responsible for their own destiny, acting under their own constitution, the Basic Law, governed by their own locally selected chief executive. In the fullness of time, they will be governed by their own elected representatives, too. Beijing's appointed organizations involved in handover preparations will be dissolved or replaced by institutions like the local Foreign Ministry office that are supposed to have only narrowly defined roles in those matters of national defense and foreign affairs that remain the legitimate purview of the central government. That leaves Hong Kong's people to face the challenges that will confront them in this new era. The outgoing colonial administration left a city in excellent working condition. But the many remaining problems will become the sole responsibility of Hong Kong people.

The good feelings engendered by the simple dignified handover, of course, will not last forever or extend into all corners of society. The domestic tussles between the "pro-Beijing" and "pro-democracy" factions will go on. It is an excellent sign that the Democratic Party, led by Martin Lee, seems committed to participating in the

Legislative Council elections scheduled for next May. The Chinese welcome their participation and are plugging a new line to the effect that allowing dissident views is actually healthy for Hong Kong. Of course, that doesn't hurt them with critics in the West. But whatever their calculations, it is encouraging that both pro-democracy and pro-Beijing forces are committed to electoral politics.

Long after the handover has faded into history, Hong Kong will remain what it has long been; the most important place where China meets and interacts with the rest of the world. That is a legacy of the colonial years. Inevitably Hong Kong will become the catalyst for wide ranging changes in China itself. Not only will the region remain the primary source of capital for the mainland's modernization, as it has been for many years, it will also be a conduit for ideas about management, finance and, shall one dare say, freedoms that will benefit the entire nation. The Joint Declaration envisioned that Hong Kong would retain its capitalist economic systems and way of life for 50 years after 1997. Before that time is up, the two systems in the mainland and SAR may have converged to such a degree that remaining differences are largely inconsequential. In fact, that may be what the wily old Deng Xiaoping had in mind when he first dreamed up "one country, two systems".

# Afterword: July 2017      +7305 DAYS

*"It's a different place."*

WHEN ANYONE ASKS me what has changed in Hong Kong in the 20 years since its return to China and the departure of the British, I usually respond that you see a lot of red flags flying (mostly the Hong Kong banner, not the PRC's), and they have painted the red Royal Mail boxes Hongkong Post green. I know that sounds rather flippant, but in fact relatively little has changed outwardly. Streetcars still trundle down streets named after colonial governors. The statue of Queen Victoria still sits in its namesake park staring placidly at the mountains. Barristers still address red judges (from the color of their gowns not their political persuasion) as "your worship". As Deng Xiaoping promised long before the handover, the dancers still dance and the horses still run.

That doesn't mean there have not been changes, even on a superficial level. Who remembers how on October 10 many parts of Hong Kong were festooned with the red and blue flag of the Republic of China. Now it would be considered politically incorrect to say the least to publicly display the *de facto* banner of Taiwan. I see other signposts when I learnt that in 2002 that colonial institution Jimmy's Kitchen had been sold to a Chinese owner. The proprietor, Neil Mackenzie, said: "Hong Kong has changed a hell of a lot in the last four or five years. . . . It's a different place. It's not a British colony any more. Jimmy's has got to be part of the Hong Kong scene rather than the expat scene."

By a strange confluence of events the Asian Financial Crisis hit exactly one day after the handover. There followed economic stagnation and high unemployment. Beijing thought it was doing Hong Kong a favor when, shortly after the handover, it permitted Chinese tourists to enter Hong Kong as individuals rather than in tour groups. That provided a needed stimulus but was to have unintended consequences further down the road.

There were other traumas in the early years such as the crash in property prices, a bird flu outbreak, scandals in the hospital administration and the deadly and frightening outbreak of SARS (Severe Acute Respiratory Syndrome) in March 2003. For months Beijing neglected to inform Hong Kong of the outbreak that was spreading rapidly in next-door Guangzhou. When a Chinese tourist brought it into Hong Kong and began infecting people it was a total shock. There was a serious loss of trust in Beijing that undermined, perhaps permanently, the good will that had accompanied the early post-handover years.

Replacing the British governor, Chief Executive Tung Chee-hwa struggled, mostly unsuccessfully, to cope with these problems. He lost the confidence of most Hong Kong people and belatedly that of Beijing too. Halfway through his second term he resigned in favor of his deputy, Donald Tsang, a career civil servant believed to be more competent and politically adept, although in retrospect he was little better than his predecessor.

As Hong Kong and China look back on the 20 years since Hong Kong reverted to Chinese sovereignty both sides find their worst fears unfounded but also their best hopes unfulfilled. Hong Kong people would, perhaps grudgingly, admit their fears that Beijing would shred their liberties have not been realized. But they are still disappointed that their hopes of full democracy, which they feel they were promised, have gone unfulfilled. In those 20 years there were few changes in the political set-up. The Legislative Council expanded to 70 seats, 40 of them decided through direct elections and 30 from specialized lists. The first two decades ended in an impasse over selection of the chief executive, now chosen by an electoral college of some 1,200 worthies, most beholden to Beijing.

For its part Beijing has to be happy that Hong Kong has not become a base for foreign subversion of the central government. But it must also be a source of deep disappointment and frustration. Hong Kong people still think of themselves as Hongkongers first and as citizens of the People's Republic of China a distant second—or third, or fourth. Polls have repeatedly underscored this trend, and no amount of morning flag-raising, exchange programs, "Love China; Love Hong Kong" drives or PLA open houses seems able to change this.

Propinquity has not improved relations between Hong Kong people and the thousands of mainland Chinese who have descended on the territory since China loosened travel restrictions—a move, as mentioned before, meant as a favor to Hong Kong. Some incidents, fairly trivial in themselves, have taken on outsized meaning. When the Italian luxury garment retailer Dolce & Gabbana opened a smart new shop on busy Canton Road in Tsim Sha Tsui, it got into trouble when the management sought to forbid locals from taking pictures of the window displays; more than 1,000 people gathered outside the store to protest.

Another irritation was the large number of pregnant Chinese women coming into the territory to have "anchor babies" allowing them to immigrate to Hong Kong but taking up limited hospital space. In one year some 40,000 mainland women gave birth in Hong Kong. One local woman told the *South China Morning Post* that she was afraid to get pregnant since she wasn't sure she could find a bed in a Hong Kong hospital. The government subsequently banned pregnant women from entering the territory.

Some 40 percent of real estate transactions are said to involve mainland buyers, boosting the profits of landlords while pricing Hong Kong people, especially those in the "sandwich class" (too well-off to apply for public housing but too poor to buy apart-ments) out. Locals find that their favorite noodle shop has closed to make way for a store selling imported watches for the Chinese tourist trade. The rise in property prices is one reason for the rapidly growing income gap, which would be a major undercurrent of many of the pro-democracy protest demonstrations later. Hong Kong had the longest "occupy" protest over inequality in the world. For 306 days in 2011–12 dozens of protesters "occupied" the public space underneath the towering HSBC Asia headquarters in

208 Farewell, My Colony

Central. In September 2012, the authorities finally moved in to clear the encampment that had lasted for many months longer than Occupy Wall Street in New York or other places in the world.

Adding to this is the notorious "locusts" advert published in *Apple Daily,* the territory's leading Chinese language newspaper. The full page ad showed a locust, presumably representing mainland China perched on a mountain top overlooking Hong Kong with the words: "Hong Kong people have had enough". Hong Kong people have a patronizing term, *Ah Chaan* that they often applied to the flood of tourists from the mainland, derived from a bumpkin-like character in a television series. It was a way that Hongkongers looked down on their poor relations to the north in the years preceding the 1997 and after the handover. They still consider mainlanders country bumpkins, only rich country bumpkins.

*    *    *    *

Hong Kong Special Administrative Region had three Chinese chief executives in its first 20 years, none of whom could capture the hearts of Hongkongers. The first CE, Tung Chee-hwa, was considered an amiable bumbler, a decent man unfortunately out of his depth. Tung showed very early that he did not possess the political skills or charisma needed to run a place like Hong Kong. There is considerable irony here. Before the handover people said that the first Chinese chief needed to be somebody economics savvy, someone highly in tune with the business community. That has been proved to be nonsense. Hong Kong has more than enough economics-savvy people. What it needed were politically agile leaders.

The second CE, Donald Tsang, seemed at first to be the perfect antidote to Tung. A self-proclaimed "typical Hong Kong boy", Tsang was born in Hong Kong (unlike Tung who was born in Shanghai) and worked his way up Hong Kong's civil service to become financial secretary and later chief secretary. His finest hour came in 1998 as financial secretary when, in the depths of the Asian financial crisis, he abruptly sacrificed *laissez faire* principles and spent billions of public money to buy stocks to shore up the Hong Kong dollar. The action saved the currency and earned the government a nice profit when the stocks were later sold. During his second term, ending 2012, however Tsang was embroiled in scandal, accused of taking gifts from tycoons in the form of trips on luxury yachts and private airplanes.

Hong Kong's third chief executive, Leung Chun-ying, universally known as "CY", never seemed to get much of a break from Hong Kong's highly politicized population. He squeaked into office after the front-runner, and Beijing-approved candidate, the then chief secretary, Henry Tang, was accused of building an illegal addition to his house. Beijing switched support to Leung who eked out a thin majority of 689 votes from the 1,200-member Election Committee. Ironically, shortly after his appointment, CY was accused of doing the same thing to his own home that got Tang into trouble.

Throughout his career he has been dogged by accusations that his first loyalty is to Beijing not Hong Kong. Some have accused him of being a closeted member of the Communist Party (curiously still illegal in Hong Kong). He has tried to alleviate some of the things that bug Hongkongers, such as the rise in property prices which he tried with little success to suppress by taxing mainlanders buying up property and banning pregnant women from entering the territory and giving birth to "anchor babies". None of these seem to have done anything to raise CY's dismal public approval ratings.

In the early days after the handover, China's leaders were more popular than Hong Kong's own, according to opinion polls. This was an era of more "moderate" Chinese leaders such as the former premier Zhu Rongji. During the big 2003 demonstration, protesters heaped abuse on Tung but did not criticize China's leaders. Premier Wen Jiabao, in Hong Kong at the time, was greeted respectfully, even warmly, everywhere he went. It is a sign how far relations had deteriorated that when Zhang Dejiang, chairman of the National People's Congress Standing Committee, visited in 2016, ostensibly to give a lecture, some 6,000 police in riot gear were deployed to provide security.

Hong Kong experienced three major crises in the 20 years since the handover. The first was the mass protest over Article 23 of the Basic Law in 2003. This time bomb obligates Hong Kong to enact laws designed to suppress "subversion" and to protect "state secrets", which are rather broadly defined in China. This article was considered so sensitive and so potentially damaging to confidence in the territory's future that the government waited five years before acting. By then, it reasoned, Hong Kong people would have become more comfortable with China and its intentions. It proved to be a serious miscalculation.

On July 1, a holiday meant to celebrate the glorious return of Hong Kong to the motherland, an estimated 500,000 people, seven percent of the population, turned out in a massive demonstration against Article 23 and the Tung administration in general. The day was hot and sunny and had a festive air. They came with their children, even babies in strollers, walking from Victoria Park to the government offices on Lower Albert Road. Aerial views on television that evening looked like a kind of tsunami of people.

In the face of such opposition, Tung withdrew the bill indefinitely. Twenty years after the handover, the government has not reintroduced the legislation, though periodically local and Beijing worthies demand that it be enacted. It was a heady exercise of people power ending in victory, and may have lulled people into thinking that future confrontations would also end so favorably. That expectation would be dashed ten years later in a larger conflict.

For 20 years since the handover, July 1 has been a public holiday. It is meant, of course, to mark and celebrate the return of Hong Kong to China after 155 years of British colonial occupation. It has become an iconic day, but not in the way that Beijing had in mind. It is no longer a day to commemorate the return to the mainland. It has become a day when people march down Hennessy Road to protest some government action or inaction. The fact that it is a public holiday also helps swell the ranks.

The second crisis in 2012 sprung from the Hong Kong government's attempt to inject greater patriotism (meaning support for the PRC) into the curriculum. The new materials included "The China Model" purported to describe the Chinese Communist Party as progressive, selfless and united while criticizing multi-party system. The decision reflected the growing frustration in Beijing that Hong Kong schools were not doing enough to foster patriotism and love of the motherland in the public schools. Opponents likened it to "brainwashing" and mobilized thousands of protesters. It was not so large as the 2003 demonstration but large enough to cause the government to backtrack and withdraw the new curriculum.

The protests over patriotic education were notable for the first appearance of the British colonial flag among the demonstrators. I almost fell off my chair in shock when I first saw a picture of the flag in the hands of some protesters on the front page of the *New York Times*. It is hard to think of anything that would be more irritating to the Chinese leaders in Beijing than for Hong Kong people to embrace the symbol of colonialism, which is officially described as 155 years of misery and oppression. The colonial flag would become even more prominent in future demonstrations.

The most serious crisis in the past 20 years was the "Umbrella Movement" of 2014, so called because the demonstrators used the umbrellas as a defense against tear gas and pepper spray (not to mention rain). The demonstrations began in September after Beijing released its proposal for electing the chief executive in 2017. It called for direct elections but retained tight control over who would be allowed to run by reserving the nominating power to the 1,200-member election committee. Opponents called it sham democracy and marched in daily street confrontations that settled down into a version of the Occupy Movement until the government removed the last barriers. The plan failed to get two-thirds majority in the Legco and was defeated.

The inconclusive ending to the Umbrella Movement left both sides in a sullen, sour mood. Beijing no longer seems to care very much about making nice with the territory. In what looked like an official reprimand, Beijing issued a "white paper" in June, 2014, (soon after the traditional memorial to the Tiananmen crackdown of 1989), saying that autonomy was not a right but something that could be revoked at any time that the central government feels its authority is threatened. There was also, in late 2015, the strange case of the five abducted Causeway Bay booksellers, which if nothing else showed that Hong Kong is no longer a safe haven for dissidents (or for foreign passport holders—one of the booksellers had a Swedish passport.)

The Umbrella Movement's failure also had some profound impact on Hong Kong's people, especially young people. They no longer seemed interested in the traditional liberal causes, such as popular election to the Legco and chief executive that had motivated their fathers for more than 20 years. Many retreated into an extreme kind of localism, being against, for example, use of Mandarin rather than the local dialect, Cantonese. They went by such names as Hong Kong Indigenous; Hong Kong Independent Party; Civic Passion, Demosisto. Some young people took part in the 2016 Lunar New Year riot in Mongkok, the most violent disturbance since the spillover of the Cultural Revolution in 1967. It seemed a long way from the halcyon days of the 2003 anti-Article 23 protests.

Time has often weighed heavily on Hong Kong. When I arrived in 1987 the handover date of 1997 seemed comfortably distant, yet the years went by in a flash. China's promise to respect Hong Kong's autonomy as a Special Administrative Region for 50 years following the handover also seemed something else in the far distant future. Yet already almost half that time has passed. Many of the young people who took part in the Umbrella Movement will be entering vigorous middle age in 2047 when the fateful year comes around. In the early years most of us assumed that Beijing would be happy to simply extend that period indefinitely. That is no longer such a certainty.

# EXPLORE ASIA WITH BLACKSMITH BOOKS

From retailers around the world or from *www.blacksmithbooks.com*